BITHELL SERIES OF DISSERTATIONS
VOLUME TWO

Figures of Transformation: Rilke and the Example of Valéry

RICHARD COX

Lecturer in French at Trinity College, Dublin

INSTITUTE OF GERMANIC STUDIES
UNIVERSITY OF LONDON 1979

ISBN 0 85457 0926

© The Institute of Germanic Studies

Printed by W. S. Maney & Son Ltd, Leeds, England
from camera copy provided by the Institute of Germanic Studies

CONTENTS

PREFACE

This book is a revised version of a Ph.D. dissertation submitted in Cambridge in 1972. I am happy to record my debt to my supervisor, Professor J.P. Stern, for unstinted assistance during the initial preparation, and continued interest thereafter, including recommendation of the dissertation for publication in this series. I am also grateful to my examiners, Professors W. McCausland Stewart and L.W. Forster, for many useful comments. It was in the nature of my subject that advice and criticism related mainly to one or other of the poets concerned, and for shortcomings in the links I have tried to establish I take of course full responsibility.

I should also like to acknowledge with thanks the generosity of Sidney Sussex College, Cambridge, for the leisure provided by a Research Fellowship during preparation of the original dissertation.

Finally, of course, I am grateful to the Institute of Germanic Studies and the Editorial Board of the Bithell Series for the opportunity to re-think my earlier conclusions, and to Mr. Corbet Stewart, acting on their behalf, for assistance and advice in revision and presentation in this form.

Dublin, 1977

REFERENCES

References to the *Duineser Elegien* are to number and line,
prefixed with E = E I,22; to the *Sonette an Orpheus* to part
and number, prefixed with S = S I,xiv. All other references
to Rilke's work are to volume and page number of the
Sämtliche Werke, edited by Ernst Zinn, 6 vols (Wiesbaden,
1955-66).

References to *La Jeune Parque* are to line number. All other
references to Valéry's work are to the *Oeuvres*, edited by
Jean Hytier, 2 vols (Paris, 1957-60).

I. INTRODUCTION

Detection of the influence of one writer on another
is a time-honoured critical pursuit. Disclaimers of such
influence on the part of the writers themselves are almost
equally commonplace. The first problem raised by Rilke's
encounter with the work of Valéry is that it offers the
unusual spectacle of a writer proclaiming a deep indebted-
ness before a largely unbelieving critical world.

The ascertainable facts concerning Rilke's reading of
Valéry, culled from letters and personal reminiscences,
have been well documented elsewhere,[1] and a brief survey
will suffice for the present purpose, which is to highlight the scope, intensity and duration of Rilke's
interest in his fellow-poet, and to note those features
which might shed light on the nature of that interest.

It has been generally assumed that Rilke's discovery
of Valéry dated from 1921. However, Claire Goll offers
the following reminiscence from 1918:

> Chaque fois que nous nous retrouvâmes, il me lisait
> des poèmes fraîchement écrits dans son petit calepin
> de poche...Un jour qu'il me lût sa traduction d'un
> fragment de la *Jeune Parque*, il s'écria extasié:
> 'Sens-tu l'étrange parenté? Valéry est venu vers moi
> comme un autre moi-même!' Et ce soir-là, il lut et
> relut le passage:
>   Je n'implorerai plus que tes faibles clartés,
>   Longtemps sur mon visage envieuse de fondre,
>   Très imminente larme...[2]

Although Mme Goll has given formal confirmation of her
dating of the occasion, her testimony remains problematical, as it predates by three years any further mention
of Valéry on Rilke's part. However, the cardinal point is
Rilke's expression of an immediate and overwhelming sense
of *affinity* with Valéry which critics have for the most
part, as will be seen, ignored or set aside.

A second aspect of Rilke's interest in Valéry - the
connexion he repeatedly made between his reading of the
French poet and the progress of his own work - is force-
fully indicated by another reminiscence, this time by
Monique St Hélier, to whom Rilke confessed:

> J'étais seul, j'attendais, toute mon oeuvre attend-
> ait. Un jour, j'ai lu Valéry, j'ai su que mon
> attente était finie.

The work in question was the cycle of Elegies, commenced
at Duino some nine years earlier, and still in a fragmentary condition. The day in question, leaving aside a possible reading of *La Jeune Parque* in 1918, was in February
of 1921, when Rilke discovered in an old (June 1920) number of the *Nouvelle Revue Française* a copy of 'Le Cimetière marin'.[4] At about the same time, he also discovered
the *Album de vers anciens*, published in 1920, and the
fragments of *Eupalinos ou l'Architecte* which appeared in
the *Nouvelle Revue française* of March 1921. His enthusiasm was instant. By the middle of March he had completed
translations of 'Le Cimetière marin' and of 'L'Amateur de
poèmes',[5] and wrote to several friends on the subject, the
most circumstantial of his letters being to André Gide,
for many years his main informant on the Parisian literary
scene:

> Mais ce n'est point à Proust que je dois mon plus
> grand étonnement pendant ces derniers mois; je ne
> saurais vous dire la profonde émotion que j'ai eue
> en lisant l'*Architecte* et (par-ci et par-là) quelques
> autres écrits de Paul Valéry. Comment est-il pos-
> sible pendant tant d'années, que je ne le connusse
> point?
>   Il y a quelques semaines j'ai traduit, en plein
> enthousiasme, ces autres 'paroles véritablement
> marines' - les strophes du *Cimetière marin*...c'est
> devenu, je crois, une de mes meilleures traductions!
> ...
>   On dirait que ce grand poète ait supprimé toutes

les formes provisoires pendant une partie de sa vie,
pour ne donner que de l'essence, tant il paraît
clair là, où la profondeur des autres ne se découvre
qu'au prix d'une certaine obscurité.

Apart from the general tone of enthusiasm, three
points may be noted about this passage. Firstly, Rilke
did not hesitate to speak of Valéry as 'ce grand poète',
before knowing of the reputation this latter was then
acquiring in France. Secondly, he speaks of the clarity
of a poem considered by many contemporary readers to be
decidedly obscure; later he was to make a similar comment
on *La Jeune Parque*, a work which has been called the most
difficult in the French language.[7] The immediacy of his
admiration and understanding support the impression gained
from Mme Goll's testimony, that is, that Rilke found in
Valéry a kindred spirit rather than a distant object of
approval. The third point to be noted is Rilke's appreci-
ation of the long gap in Valéry's career as poet, and his
interpretation of that silence as a long process of
maturation. No doubt he had already made that comparison
between Valéry's 'grand silence' and his own relative
silence over the previous decade which was to become a
constant theme of his comments on Valéry.

His letter was not wasted on Gide, one of Valéry's
oldest and most consistent friends, who not only declared
himself enchanted with it, but also showed it to Valéry
himself. Via Gide, Valéry mentioned his wish to see
translated into German the new preface he had written for
his *Léonard de Vinci*, and Rilke's reply is interesting
for its cautious tone:

> Aussitôt que le calme sera un peu rétabli chez moi,
> je ferai quelques essais de traduction pour me
> rendre compte, si je dispose des moyens à donner des
> équivalents précis de *Note et digression*; du premier

coup je ne suis pas sûr de ma capacité et (devant
vous il est permis que je le dise), l'*Architecte*
m'attire tout autrement, quoique là aussi les
difficultés seraient considérables; - mais peut-être
qu'elles soient plus dans ma ligne.[8]

Similarly, whilst writing of the 'étonnante poésie' of the
'Ébauche d'un serpent', he suggests that he does not find
it as congenial as the 'Cimetière marin'.[9]

In July of 1920, the three poems 'Aurore', 'La
Pythie' and 'Palme' were published together under the
title *Odes*, and in a letter to Marie von Thurn und Taxis
Rilke quoted from 'Palme' with a comment which was to become common in his correspondence:

In seinem Gedichte 'Palme' steht:
    Patience, patience,
    patience dans l'azur!
    Chaque atome de silence
    est la chance d'un fruit mûr!
(Könnt ich das auch für mein Schweigen erhoffen.)[10]

December of 1921 brought the first direct communica-
tion between the two poets in the shape of a letter from
Valéry to Rilke. Couched in a characteristically reserved
style, it elicited a characteristic response from Rilke,
who copied the entire letter for Merline; his comments to
her and to Gide border on effusiveness.[11] The extent of
Rilke's involvement with the work of Valéry by this stage
may be gauged from the fact that in the same month he
declined Gide's request for a translation of *Les Nourritures terrestres*, urging the pressure of his own work and
of his translations of Michelangelo.[12] These had not pre-
vented him, and did not in the future prevent him, from
translating Valéry. Though Rilke did not say so, Gide -
a close literary acquaintance through many years - had
been eclipsed in a matter of months.

More remarkably still, Rilke's own work did not eclipse his interest in Valéry. Between 2 and 23 February 1922 he completed the *Duineser Elegien* and wrote the *Sonette an Orpheus* in one of the most sustained bursts of creativity known to literary history. Writing on 9 February to announce to Merline - a little prematurely - the completion of the Elegies, he sent her a copy of *L'Ame et la danse*, made *in his own hand*.[13] Indeed, reading the correspondence of this extraordinary period, one has the almost absurd impression that this storm of composition was a passing moment in a phase dedicated principally to the reading of Valéry. For Christmas, 1921, Rilke had chosen to send Merline a copy of the introduction to La Fontaine's *Adonis*;[14] in February came the manuscript of *L'Ame et la danse* already mentioned, followed at Easter by a copy of the 'Ébauche d'un serpent'.[15] Some time in February or March of 1922 he obtained a copy of the *Soirée avec M. Teste* which he had been seeking for a year;[16] a letter written shortly afterwards characterizes Valéry as 'den Dichter, dem unter den Franzosen meiner Generation meine größte und staunende Bewunderung gehört'.[17] References to Valéry are fewer in the summer of 1922, but this was in many ways an unproductive time,[18] and with Rilke's retreat into the solitude of Muzot at the onset of winter they become more frequent even than before. In response to a request for advice on contemporary authors, Rilke singled out Valéry as the most significant of a list which included French, English and German writers.[19] In December, he recommended Valéry's poetry and prose to his Polish translator as fit subjects for wider dissemination.[20] By Christmas he had several translations from *Charmes* ready for Merline, and in the New Year wrote to Katherina Kippenberg of his intention of spending the winter 'in meiner Stille, ganz Übersetzungen gewidmet'.[21] His

letters of the next few months are indeed full of references to work in this field, and by the end of April he
was engaged in copying out his translations into a large
leather-bound volume to be sent to Valéry as a quasi-
devotional offering.[22]

Some mention may be made in passing of the personal
relationships between the two poets. They met for the
first time in April 1924, at Sierre; it is difficult to
gauge the tenor of this encounter either from the laconic
postcard Valéry sent to his wife,[23] or from Rilke's
description of the occasion as 'eine sehr sondere
Begegnung'.[24] In January of 1925, in a moment of revolt
against his worsening physical condition, Rilke escaped
to Paris, but Valéry was busy with his candidature to the
Académie, and the two appear to have met only infre-
quently. Maurice Betz has suggested that Rilke did not
find Valéry as cordial as he had hoped.[25] A meeting in
September 1926 appears to have restored the fabric of
their personal relationship, but it seems that Valéry did
not realize Rilke's poetic stature until after his death,
when he paid generous tribute. Since he had no German,
his view of Rilke was of course coloured by what was
available in translation; a photograph taken of Valéry's
work-table at his death in 1945 features the French
translation of *Das Buch von der Armut und vom Tode*.[26]

On Rilke's side, however, there was no diminution of
admiration and active dissemination; one of the fullest
discussions of Valéry's work dates from as late as February of 1926. The most interesting aspect of this account
lies in the difference Rilke notes between his reading of
the *Soirée avec M. Teste* and that of *La Jeune Parque*.
Of the first he writes:

Was mich angeht, so habe ich an die zwei Jahre vor
dem Teste-Problem gestanden ohne den Eingang zu
finden, in den unerhörten kleinen Tempel...Endlich,
durch die inneren inkommensurabeln Verschiebungen
in der eigenen Natur vorbereitet, kam der Tag, da
ich die Feier des Eintritts mir gewährt fand – und
seither ist meine Bewunderung für das unbeschreib-
liche kleine Buch, das sich zeilenlang ins völlig
Unbetretene niederschreibt, immer noch gewachsen.

Of his reading of the poem, however, he claims:

Ich verstand dieses Gedicht der Gedichte...im ersten
(Vor-)Lesen, vom Blatt weg.[27]

In the case of both texts, however, the account is a very
personal one, whereas the praise of the *Introduction à la
méthode de Léonard de Vinci*, though generous, is more distant. Warmth returns with the mention of translations of
Eupalinos and *L'Ame et la danse* as projects long delayed
but still close to his heart.

It was not until a matter of weeks before his death
that Rilke was able to write to his publisher announcing
the completion of these translations.[28] But even that was
not the end of his translating activity. By November, his
final illness was closing in, but having engaged the ser-
vices of a young Russian secretary, he dictated a version
of *Tante Berthe*, the last published work of his life-
time.[29] Appropriately, the last letter of this dedicated
letter-writer concludes with a reference to Valéry and to
'notre profonde relation'.[30]

*   *   *   *   *   *   *   *

What then, were the terms of that 'profonde relation'? Although Rilke left no single detailed account of
his interest in Valéry, certain features can be discerned
from the letters and reminiscences surveyed.

Firstly, the scope of his interest was wide, covering

works of many different kinds. By the time of his death,
he possessed copies of the *Album de vers anciens*, *Charmes*,
La Jeune Parque, *Eupalinos*, *L'Ame et la danse*, *La Soirée
avec M. Teste* (with such of its pendants as had by then
appeared), *L'Introduction à la méthode de Léonard de
Vinci*, *Note et digression*, *Au sujet d'Adonis*, the 1924
edition of *Variété*, the *Fragment d'un Descartes*, the
Entretiens of Lefèvre, *Une Conquête méthodique*, *Rhumbs*,
Le Retour d'Hollande, *Tante Berthe*, *Analecta* and *De la
diction des vers*.[31]

Secondly, certain works from that list were singled
out for special attention, notably the poems of maturity,
the Socratic dialogues with a particular predilection for
L'Ame et la danse, and, after initial incomprehension and
rather late in life, the *Soirée avec M. Teste*.

Thirdly, that initial appearance of undiscriminating
admiration concealing an insistent personal selectivity is
mirrored in the general tone of his comments on Valéry.
On the one hand, he placed Valéry almost from the outset
on a pedestal, as first among his contemporaries; he wrote
to him and of him in quasi-devotional terms, sometimes to
an embarrassing extent. His response to Valéry's 'grand
silence' at times implies a certain self-condemnation for
his own failure to suppress 'toutes les formes provisoires'. At the same time, he seems to have been
capable of being aggrieved that Valéry did not recognize
his achievement and importance; he re-interprets his own
silence as a process of maturation rather than a dis-
ability; and privately, he was prepared to claim a
'parenté', a 'profonde relation' rather than a pious
humility, to see Valéry as 'un autre moi-même'.

Attempts to interpret Rilke's attitude to Valéry have

generally taken a more simplistic line. Whether in
general biographical and critical studies of Rilke, or
in works specifically devoted to the relationships between
Rilke and French writers, emphasis has been placed almost
unanimously on the *dissimilarity* of the two poets, usually
seen as the basis of Rilke's admiration, as in Hartmann
Goertz's conclusion:

> Valéry und Rilke sind reine Gegensätze, und ihre
> starke Anziehungskraft liegt gerade in dieser
> Gegensätzlichkeit begründet.[32]

Or, as Marga Bauer puts it, directly contradicting Rilke's
own words,

> Das Fremdeste zieht ihn an, denn er will im andern
> Menschen nicht das Ich, sondern das Du, an dem er
> steigen, emporwachsen kann.[33]

The sharp contrasts drawn between the two poets rest most
commonly on an (excessively summary) analysis of personal
temperament and modes of inspiration, confusing the forms
of creative imagination with its effects, as in Bauer's
characterization of Valéry as 'diese kühle, fremde,
glasartige Erscheinung'.[34] Furthermore, even if it were
possible to accept as generally valid Angelloz's drastic-
ally simplified picture of Valéry as 'un logicien épris
de recherche rationelle', occupied with 'une analyse
impitoyablement lucide', [35] Rilke's incomprehension of the
Soirée avec M. Teste, his preference for *Eupalinos* as
against *Léonard de Vinci*, and for *L'Ame et la danse* as
against *Eupalinos*, for 'Le Cimetière Marin' as against
'Ébauche d'un serpent', all suggest that *his* picture was
rather consciously designed to play down that aspect of
Valéry's literary personality.

Emphasis on the dissimilarity between the two poets conforms also rather too neatly to the general heading - that of 'Rilke and France' - under which Rilke's encounter with Valéry has been most commonly discussed, most fully in two relatively recent works by Charles Dédéyan and K.A.J. Batterby.[36] The latter's work has much detailed commentary and discussion of a highly valuable kind, but the interpretation of Rilke's interest in Valéry is determined in advance by the central thesis of the book, in which the over-schematic views of critics already quoted are writ large in the picture of the French writer as 'the practitioner *par excellence* of the logical approach, of clear, rational analysis and exposition', assisting Rilke to overcome 'his natural antipathy to any formal discipline'.[37] Now it would be perverse to deny that at an earlier stage of Rilke's career, the notion of 'France' as an ideal symbol of clarity, control and form, in contradistinction not only to Germany, but also to Russia and to Scandinavia, held some sway in his mind. But in the period with which we are concerned, Rilke's acquaintance with the French literary scene was extraordinarily extensive, and it seems improbable that he would still have thought in such terms. Given his admiration for Francis Jammes or (if one thinks of writers in the French *language*) the Belgians Emile Verhaeren and Maurice Maeterlinck, none of whom could remotely be considered as practitioners of clear, rational analysis, it is clear that Rilke's interest in any particular French writer must be taken on its merits. It is not at all difficult to see what Rilke admired in these writers - and in each case the admiration is a form of fellow-feeling rather than discipleship; Jammes's celebration of the traditional, Verhaeren's vision of 'les villes tentaculaires' and Maeterlinck's celebration of the virtues of *silence*, must all have found a ready response. There is no reason to

10

suppose that Rilke's admiration for Valéry is not of a
similar variety, grounded in the first instance, however
far it went beyond, in a recognition of affinity; and the
best indicator remains his personal choice among Valéry's
texts.

If critics have not been noticeably successful in
explaining Rilke's initial attraction to Valéry, it is
even more doubtful whether any coherent account has yet
been produced of the impact of his reading on his own
work. His statement to Monique St. Hélier that the completion of his work was due to his reading of Valéry has
generally been interpreted as a reference to the
encouragement he took from Valéry's years of silence.
Von Salis writes:

> Die Bedeutung, die Paul Valéry für Rainer Maria Rilke
> in seinen fünf, sechs letzten Lebensjahren besaß,
> kann nicht genug hervorgehoben werden...Am stärksten
> betroffen, weil an seiner wundesten Stelle berührt,
> war Rilke, als er erfuhr, daß der französische
> Dichter erst nach einem viele Jahre währenden,
> völligen Schweigen mit seinen Gedichten hervorge-
> treten war![38]

Of Rilke's reception of the commendation of patient matur-
ing found in 'Palme', Renée Lang comments:

> Ces vers de 'Palme' agirent sur lui comme le via-
> tique administré à un pieux malade; 'Puissé-je
> aussi espérer une telle chose pour mon silence',
> écrivit-il à une de ses correspondentes'.[39]

All this is undoubtedly true. But without some sense on
Rilke's part that the works which finally emerged from
Valéry's silence were in some way peculiarly valuable,
the example could scarcely have been so effective.
Everything about Rilke's interest in Valéry - the immedi-
acy of his understanding of *La Jeune Parque*, his active

work of translation and propaganda (continuing long after
the completion of the Elegies), his determination to seek
understanding of the *Soirée* - argues a deep concern for
the *content* of these texts, and not merely for their manner of production.

If the reading of Valéry were indeed of such profound
importance for the works of February 1922, one might
reasonably expect to be able to trace some kind of evidence within the works themselves. The works of Batterby
and Dédéyan illustrate two approaches to this possibility.
For Batterby, the impact of Valéry's work on Rilke is to
be located above all in language, in the 'terseness', the
'extreme, almost elliptical economy' of Valéry's poetry,
contributing to Rilke's synthesis in Elegies and Sonnets
of the best elements in French and German.[40] The argument
is not, I think, to be dismissed entirely. But it is
difficult to take it as either conclusive or comprehensive.
In the first case, it depends on the identification of a
significant stylistic shift between the 1912-15 Elegies
and those added in 1922 - a shift which (to me) is not by
any means convincingly demonstrated - and on a rather imprecise use of terms such as 'terseness' and 'economy' to
relate the measured, quasi-classical cadences of Valéry's
decasyllables and Alexandrines to Rilke's tense, often
staccato *vers libre*, with its abrupt changes of mood and
register. In the second place, it is an argument difficult to reconcile with Rilke's equally passionate dedication to the sinuous, often digressive prose and generally
loose structure of the Socratic dialogues. Again, one is
driven back to the *content* of Valéry's texts.

Dédéyan is nothing if not bold in his assessment of
influence at the level of content. All those Elegies and
sections of Elegies written in 1922, he claims, were

written 'sous le coup de Paul Valéry'. Thus he compares
the closing lines of the fifth Elegy with sections from
L'Ame et la danse, and asks:

> Or n'est-ce pas Valéry qui a enseigné à Rilke que
> l'art symbolique, la danse, peut rendre l'essence
> et l'âme des choses et de l'univers?[41]

In view of the fact that the lines in question derive
directly from the opening of the Elegy, with its picture
of the 'Saltimbanques', and that the inspiration for that
imagery is universally acknowledged to derive from the
painting by Picasso, if not from Baudelaire's poem and
from memories of Père Rollin's troupe, mentioned in
letters of 1907,[42] it is clear that the question need not
be taken rhetorically. Later, Dédéyan writes:

> Valéry l'invitait dans le 'Cimetière marin' à cette
> conception de la vie, qui reprenait en épigraphe la
> phrase de Pindare: 'O mon âme, n'aspire pas à
> l'immortalité, mais épuise le champs du possible.'
> Ainsi la mort aura pour contrepoids et pour compensa-
> tion l'art, qui est la réalisation du possible.
> Rilke n'est plus obsédé par l'Inconnaissable, par
> l'idée d'anéantissement; grâce à Valéry, il s'appuie
> sur son élan poétique, transformant le *visible* en
> *invisible*, le *physique* en *psychique*, selon les leçons
> de la psychologie valéryenne. N'est-ce pas ce que
> nous voyons dans les Elégies?[43]

Such bare assertions raise more problems than they solve.
It is difficult to believe that Valéry would have recognized either the notion of art as compensation for death
as the 'doctrine' of 'Le Cimetière marin', or the elegiac
transformation of visible into invisible as being in
accordance with his 'leçons de psychologie'.

With regard to the Sonnets, there is more general
agreement, and indeed more precise evidence. In particular,

the association of the sonnets I.xiii ('Voller Apfel,
Birne und Banane'), I.xiv ('Wir gehen um mit Blume,
Weinblatt, Frucht'), and I.xv ('Wartet..., das schmeckt')
with certain sections of 'Le Cimetière marin' ('Comme le
fruit se fond en jouissance'), and of sonnets II.xii
('Wolle die Wandlung') and II.x ('Tänzerin: o du Verlegung') with sections of *L'Ame et la danse*, is made by
several critics. In the first instance the association
is undeniable, but trivial, since Valéry's simile is little
more than incidental; furthermore, equally convincing
parallels have been drawn between those sonnets which re-
use Valéry's image and a work which Rilke knew well before
he had even heard of Valéry - Gide's *Nourritures
terrestres*.[44] The other *rapprochement* is more interesting,
particularly in the comparison of

> Wolle die Wandlung. O sei für die Flamme
> begeistert,
> drin sich ein Ding dir entzieht, das mit
> Verwandlungen prunkt...

and

> Mais qu'est-ce qu'une flamme, ô mes amis, si ce n'est
> *le moment même?* - Ce qu'il y a de fol, et de joyeux,
> et de formidable dans l'instant même!...Flamme est
> l'acte de ce moment qui est entre la terre et le ciel.
> O mes amis, tout ce qui passe de l'état lourd à l'etat
> subtil passe par le moment de feu et de lumière...
> (II,171)

But none of the critics who draw this comparison exploit
its interest. To establish such a parallel is not *of itself* of any particular significance; unless one is merely
interested in convicting an author of plagiarism or in
demonstrating the possibility that he read other authors'
works, borrowed imagery is simply a useful first indication. In the case of 'Wolle die Wandlung', any use of the
sonnet to establish a claim of influence in the simple
cause-and-effect model has to contend with the

unmistakeable fact that, as Erich Heller puts it,

> almost every word - 'Wandlung', 'Flamme', 'jener
> entwerfende Geist, welcher das Irdische meistert',
> 'was sich ins Bleiben verschließt, schon ists das
> Erstarrte', 'Hammer' and 'Härtestes' - belongs as
> its most unmistakeable property to Zarathustra's
> prophetic household.[45]

It has to contend with the general consensus of opinion
that Rilke's poetic world was firmly fixed before his reading of Valéry. It has to contend with the particular
nature of Rilke's poetic development, as characterized for
instance by Goertz:

> Rilkes organisches, innerlich begründetes Wachstum
> entzieht sich dem harten und oft vergewaltigenden
> Begriff des Einflusses ganz, und wirklich Über-
> nommenes gehört alsbald zu seinen eigenen Erfahrungen,
> ja wurde wohl durch sie erst überhaupt gefunden, so
> daß Einheit und Selbständigkeit seines Werkes niemals
> von außen berührt oder unterbrochen werden konnte.[46]

To make sense of the comparison of two fragments of text,
in other words, more is required than simple *rapprochement*.
Even an investigation of the function of a particular image
in Rilke's work will not necessarily provide adequate
grounds for conclusion; Dietgard Kramer-Lauff's painstaking
examination of the motif of dance in Rilke's work still
leaves open, in a brief appendix, the question of a possible
connexion between the Sonnet 'Tänzerin: o du Verlegung' and
L'Ame et la danse.[47] Without some sense of the function of
images of flame and dance in the Sonnets as a whole, and
without some account of the place of the Sonnets in Rilke's
work as a whole, and particularly in relation to the Elegies,
it is impossible to determine whether Rilke's re-use of
Valéry's images is a trivial and isolated borrowing, or a
clue to the meaning of his words to Monique St. Hélier:

'Un jour, j'ai lu Valéry, j'ai su que mon attente était finie'.

*   *   *   *   *   *   *   *

The myopic vision of an older school of *comparatistes* contrasts strongly with the godlike view of the modern thematic critic, professing a fine disdain for the positivistic naiveté of 'influence' and for the minutiae of an individual poetic career. Geoffrey Hartman places both Rilke and Valéry in a motionless, artificially flattened landscape - faintly Genevan-phenomenological in topology - in close company with Wordsworth and Hopkins;[48] Priscilla Washburn Shaw constructs a neatly balanced, if equally static triangle between Rilke, Valéry and Yeats.[49] It will be apparent from subsequent pages how much the present work owes to both operations - in the case of Hartman's at least the result is an abiding part of our critical scene - but, like much of the best of modern criticism, the procedures involved require a severe amputation of the quiddities of the individual case. Their partially contrasting conclusions - Hartman seeing the two poets as 'related by their effort to gain pure representation through the direct sensuous intuition of reality',[50] Shaw drawing a bold contrast between them in respect of the relationships implicit in their works between the self and reality - are only possible, I think, because of the scant respect paid by either critic to the possibility of substantial change and development within the careers of the two poets. The two *oeuvres* are treated for the most part as if they were synchronic unities, born fully-armed from the head of the *Zeitgeist*, in which perspective changes of emphasis, intensification of tensions, later resolutions and partial resolutions, revaluations of aspirations and concerns disappear from view.

The act of comparison may be seen as the seeking of a
single perspective in which two otherwise dissimilar phenomena come to be viewed as possessing nonetheless a certain affinity; the comparison of *literary* phenomena tends
to the odious to the extent that the chosen perspective is
substituted with too great a degree of finality for the
irreducible unity of the single *oeuvre*. Detection of
'influence' - when it crosses the boundaries of genre or
language, and thus escapes the anxiety of *Epigonentum* analysed by Harold Bloom - is in itself a trivial pursuit of
the arbitrary, of what might easily have been otherwise.
But the interplay of affinity and influence holds a certain promise. Echoes of Valéry's world abound in Rilke's
late poetry, but transmuted into something rich and strange.
The analysis, not in the first place of influence, but of
the affinity which made it possible, casts a certain light
on Rilke's work - a light which we do well to examine precisely because it is in some sense Rilke's. In this wary
age, we may well suspect the poet's own explicit statements
about his poetry; but his admiration for another, freely
elected writer, hailed as 'un autre moi-même' may well be
the nearest we can get to Rilke's own 'reading' of his
works. At the same time, a certain system of checks and
balances is possible. The critic, as third party with less
at stake, whilst attempting as best he can to articulate the
unspoken dialogue between the two, observes at the same time
the shifts of emphasis, the sometimes radical changes in
tone, which accompany, or perhaps even constitute, one
poet's assimilation of the other's words. Valéry's own
observations on the subject come close to our purpose:

> Il n'est pas de mot qui vienne plus aisément ni plus
> souvent sous la plume de la critique que le mot
> d'*influence*, et il n'est point de notion plus vague
> parmi les vagues notions qui composent l'armement
> illusoire de l'esthétique. Rien toutefois dans
> l'examen de nos productions qui intéresse plus

philosophiquement l'intellect et le doive plus exciter
à l'analyse que cette modification progressive d'un
esprit par l'oeuvre d'un autre.
   Il arrive que l'oeuvre de l'un reçoive dans l'être
d'un autre une valeur toute singulière, y engendre des
conséquences agissantes qu'il était impossible de
prévoir et qui se font assez souvent impossibles à
déceler. (I,634)

With such a warning in mind, the tactic here has been therefore to alternate an emphasis on convergent points with an
emphasis on the internal unity and progress of Rilke's work.
Commencing with a close examination of a single short poem
by each poet as a means of establishing the general perspective of comparison, earlier configurations from each *oeuvre*
are called in to redress the balance, both to provide a
background to those poems, and to highlight the differences
between the poets within that general perspective. Certain
features of Rilke's work which appear especially important
in this respect are then charted through his work to the
point where he read Valéry; those works of Valéry for which
Rilke professed greatest admiration are then examined in
turn; and finally Rilke's later work is scrutinized in the
double perspective of his own earlier work and of Valéry's
works. It is hoped that, by this method, the convergences
which emerge will be given due recognition, but will be
constantly replaced in the general framework of Rilke's
development, whilst that framework itself will stand out the
clearer for the suggested comparisons and contrasts.

   I have tried to bear in mind that most readers of this
book will be more familiar with Rilke than with Valéry, and
have thus tried to present an account of Valéry, with ample
quotation, which will not rely too heavily on extensive
previous knowledge. It should be remembered that the
account which results from the perspective adopted is both
coloured in emphasis by Rilke's own selectivity, and

truncated by the thirty years which separate the period of
Rilke's encounter and Valéry's own death. With these
reservations, it is not, I think, noticeably unorthodox,
although it emphasizes to a greater degree than is commonly
the case the existential roots of Valéry's philosophical
enterprise; no under-estimation of the independent interest
of that enterprise is intended.

As for Rilke, it is doubtful whether a current 'ortho-
doxy' exists; again, however, I have found it necessary to
emphasize the directly existential nature of Rilke's concerns, and equally, no undervaluing of other perspectives
is implied. In either case, I have refrained for the most
part from engaging in detailed controversy over specific
points, except where a particularly crucial issue is most
easily crystallized by reference to previous critical work.
Otherwise, specialists will no doubt recognize points of
agreement or disagreement with generally accepted interpretations, and I can only hope that the disagreements do not
seem merely eccentric. The decision to limit discussion to
a small group of major texts was imposed, in the case of
Valéry, by the attempt to follow Rilke's own reading. In
the case of Rilke, concentration on the major collections,
with relatively brief reference to the wealth of other
material, corresponds to a belief that the notion of a
collection mattered to Rilke himself, a point discussed
later at greater length. My general approach to Rilke is
perhaps critical, but not censorious, as seems to me the
case with some recent work. If such an attitude is characteristic of a typically Anglo-Saxon tradition of Rilke-
criticism, it may be no matter for accusations of parochial-
ism. Criticism from a viewpoint other than that of the
national tradition to which the poet himself belongs adds
only a further dimension to that balance of empathy and
'Gegenübersein' which characterizes the critical act - as
it characterized Rilke's reading of Valéry.

II. TWO POEMS

'Les Pas' and 'Atmen, du unsichtbares Gedicht'

Tes pas, enfants de mon silence,
Saintement, lentement placés,
Vers le lit de ma vigilance
Procèdent muets et glacés.

Personne pure, ombre divine,
Qu'ils sont doux, tes pas retenus!
Dieux!... tous les dons que je devine
Viennent à moi sur ces pieds nus!

Si, de tes lèvres avancées,
Tu prépares pour l'apaiser,
A l'habitant de mes pensées
La nourriture d'un baiser,

Ne hâte pas cet acte tendre,
Douceur d'être et de n'être pas,
Car j'ai vécu de vous attendre
Et mon coeur n'était que vos pas. (I,120)

The capacity of Valéry's shorter poems to entice and
elude at the same moment and thus to provoke in the reader,
despite their apparently luminous verbal surface, a sense
of mild disorientation, is mirrored in the exegetical con-
tentiousness which surrounds 'Les Pas'. For J.R. Lawler,
interpreting *Charmes* as a whole as a series of marginalia
on the sustained effort of composition which lay behind *La
Jeune Parque*, the poem is concerned above all with a drama
of the creative sensibility faced with a rhythm which, like
that of the decasyllabic line which Valéry claimed to have
been the 'onlie begetter' of 'Le Cimetière marin', obsesses
the poet, but requires to be married to a sense to produce
the completed poem.[51] For others, more flatly, the

'personne pure' represents inspiration. Such an interpretation was dismissed by the poet himself as part of a
'tissu d'hypothèses et d'explications imaginaires' surrounding what he himself described as a 'petit poème purement
sentimental'.[52] Yet he was also prepared to write 'mes vers
ont le sens qu'on leur prête' (I,1509), and the poem has
been lent other senses than the 'sentimental', with a degree
of reasonableness which fails to carry conviction only to
the extent that they threaten to reduce the overt situation,
with its attendant sensuality, to mere cipher. 'Un beau
vers renaît indéfiniment de ces cendres' (I,1510) - reduced
to the interpretation it seems to invite, the poem is reborn
to further life, other possibilities.

Disagreement arises to the extent that exegesis centres
on the identification of the mysterious figure whose steps
provide the title. Muse or mistress? The problem is mis-
placed, for although it is implicitly posed - as Valéry's
own laconic formula suggests, one cannot abstract the way a
poem actually has been read - it is deliberately not
answered. 'Aux meilleurs esprits/Que d'erreurs promises!'
The poem is entitled 'Les Pas' - and not 'Anne' like an
earlier poem, or even 'La Distraite', like a later; its
centre of gravity lies not in the owner of the 'pieds nus'-
who remains, as it were, out of focus, known only in distant
forms of address as 'personne pure, ombre divine'- but in
the consciousness of her approach. It is the speaker's reactions we follow, his mounting expectations and hesitations
that we share. Indeed, it is out of his silence that the
steps are born. That is not to say that the event which the
poem recreates is in any simple sense purely internal, for
that silence itself, the vigilance, the very contours of the
waiting consciousness, have been shaped around the approaching steps: 'Et mon coeur n'était que vos pas'. But the
object which creates the inner disturbance is less important

in the poem than the disturbance itself; the poem directs
our attention to the ripples, not the stone.

Tactically imprecise at one level, the poem has its own
precision on its own terms. The unfulfilled expectation
urges the reader to take it as offering, not the quiddities
of the specific, but a pattern of experience. Valéry found
no higher praise for his first master Mallarmé than that he
had sought an algebra to replace the arithmetic of earlier
poets,[53] and it is perhaps legitimate to describe 'Les Pas'
as an algebraic formula of a certain type of experience, an
expectant attentiveness whose delights and hesitations
remain identical whatever its object. Valéry's poems,
Christine Crow observes, are concerned less with 'tracing
the development of experience along a horizontal axis' than
with finding the point of view of 'maximum generality'.[54]

What then, in terms of this 'maximum generality', is
the pattern of experience that the poem presents? Not, as
has already been suggested, one of purely inner experience,
but rather the inner effects of an encounter with the outer.
In the images of the first and last lines, the two poles
are delicately balanced, but the overt sense of the final
sentence - the invitation 'not to hasten' - combines with
the change from intimate 'tu' to formal 'vous' to suggest
a movement of withdrawal even in the moment of consummation.
The threshold of being and not-being - 'Douceur d'être et de
n'être pas' - is reached in a movement of passive submission which is however already overtaken by a counter-
vailing movement towards detachment, savouring the moment
as if from the outside, and reflecting on the experience in
the past tenses of the last two lines. The moment of consummation is also one of a profound modification of the
self in its inner dynamics, but another self observes the
change. 'Gestures of relationship between the self and the

world' is one critic's description of *Charmes*[55] - gestures
not from a distance, however, but provoked by an intimate
merging and re-separation, the outer disturbance born of
the poet's silence, the self shaping itself momentarily to
that disturbance. Gestures which retain, moreover, a sense
of profound 'courtoisie' in the dialectic represented here
in miniature, the *rhythm* of relationship between our inmost
sense of self and the world of experience.

     *   *   *   *   *   *   *   *

    In the first Sonnet of the second part of the *Sonette
an Orpheus*, J.B. Leishman observes, one might detect, 'or
fancy that one detects, some affinity with Paul Valéry':[56]

> Atmen, du unsichtbares Gedicht!
> Immerfort um das eigne
> Sein rein eingetauschter Weltraum. Gegengewicht,
> in dem ich mich rhythmisch ereigne.
>
> Einzige Welle, deren
> allmähliches Meer ich bin;
> sparsamstes du von allen möglichen Meeren, -
> Raumgewinn.
>
> Wieviele von diesen Stellen der Räume waren schon
> innen in mir. Manche Winde
> sind wie mein Sohn.
>
> Erkennst du mich, Luft, du, voll noch einst
>   meiniger Orte?
> Du, einmal glatte Rinde,
> Rundung und Blatt meiner Worte.

    As with many of Rilke's later works, the reader is
perhaps most immediately struck by a language which could
be described as passionately abstract. Few poets could use
abstract nouns like 'Sinn', 'Weltraum' or 'Raumgewinn', or
use an impersonal verb like 'sich ereignen' with a personal
subject, with such complete persuasiveness of the fact that
they translate, not purely intellectual concepts, but
passionately lived experience. Where Valéry suggests
abstraction in a poem whose overt sense is of a purely

sentimental order, Rilke infuses the abstract with powerful currents of feeling. But even if passionate, abstrac-
tions suggest pattern rather than quiddity, and Rilke's
sonnet announces more directly than the French poem the
generality of its concern. Indeed, the choice of the
structuring metaphor of the poem, the intimate physical
act of breathing, to provide a symbolic filling-out of its
abstract algebra, seems almost mannered, saved from
preciousness by the sheer intensity of the emotional logic.

The slight ambiguity of inner and outer which makes
Valéry's poem so teasing is pre-empted here by the immediate
announcement of an exchange of being between the two. But
the terms of that exchange are no less subtle than those
mediated through Valéry's unobtrusive syntax. It is not
only 'against' - as implied by the image of 'Gegengewicht' -
but *in* the exchange of self and world-space that the self
finds its 'rhythmical realisation' (in Leishman's phrase).
This slight distortion of the obvious sense of the metaphor
has far-reaching implications which the sonnet progressively
unfolds; immediately however it leads into the more intimate
metaphor of the second quatrain. Contrary perhaps to the
reader's expectations, it is the self which is the sea, and
a sea which, again with a nuancing of everyday sense, accumu-
lates its waves in a frugal garnering of 'Weltraum' within
itself. The context, together with the previous use of the
word 'Raum', forces a morphological decomposition of 'Raumgewinn', obscuring the normal sense in favour of a notion of
'profit in space'. The nature of this profit is the burden
of the tercets, which open with a Rilkean version of Valéry's
'enfants de mon silence' in the deduction from the exchange
of inner and outer that the winds are sons of the self. The
pleonasm of 'innen in mir' suggests the intimacy of the exchange, no mere contact of surfaces, but a relationship of
inner depths to the outer ubiquity of space. Profit to the

self, therefore, in the sense that it is surrounded, not by an alien element, but by something literally its own. The recognition solicited in the final tercet is thus not only an acknowledgement of acquaintance, but of status - as both creator and garnerer of space. And the acknowledgement is returned in the final lines - which suggest more than the obvious statement that air, in the form of breath, is the medium of our speech. The poem commenced with a description of breathing as 'unsichtbares Gedicht' - a formulation characteristically Rilkean in illuminating the vehicle as well as the tenor of the metaphor, in suggesting, that is, that a poem, like breathing, is a form of rhythmical exchange between inner and outer. The 'words' of the conclusion are thus more than the passage of the air through the larynx; they are the shapes of experience, moulded out of the inner life by the pressure of the outer. The self is like a tree whose roundness and enclosing bark are created by the experience of its environment.

In Rilke's, as in Valéry's poem, then, the dialectic of inner and outer is complete. But if equally achieved and harmonious in the two cases, it has subtly different shapes and scope. In the first case, the image chosen by Rilke admits of no movement of withdrawal comparable to that which closes 'Les Pas', for the recognition of the self which the sonnet celebrates is a function of its rôle in a system of exchange. Paradoxically, it is Valéry's poem, not Rilke's, which incarnates more fully the logical sense of the metaphor of 'Gegengewicht', which leaves the reader with the impression of two delicately balanced but finally distinct poles of force. To be more explicit, it reveals a sense of a self in control, able to savour its modifications by the world of experience precisely because some part of it remains detached and unmodified, whereas the exchanges of Rilke's poem are 'pure', the entire self being given up in

25

the diastole of the rhythm. But equally, the systolic
movement of Rilke's poem is also all-embracing, comprehend-
ing the entire world of space. While Valéry's poem moves
between two thresholds, marking out the limited boundaries
of the human experience between the extremes of self-
enclosure and passivity, Rilke's marries a total abandonment
to an all-embracing claim, a sense of relatedness at once
cosmic and intimate between self and natural world.

    Analysis of single poems is apt, beyond a certain
point, to become precariously conjectural. Moreover, the
two poems in question here are mature, achieved harmonies,
behind which lie in either case long and patient explorations of tensions late and recently resolved. Consideration
of these tensions offers firstly a less speculative understanding of the affinities and contrasts glimpsed in 'Les
Pas' and the Orpheus Sonnet, as prelude to an attempt to
chart that complex process by which the resolution of
Valéry's mature work, apprehended by Rilke with a mixture of
insight and selective emphasis, and subjected to a revisionary 'Steigerung', could become the catalyst for the *Sonette
an Orpheus*.

III. STRATEGIES OF NUANCE AND PARADOX

Rilke's work from *Erste Gedichte* to *Die Aufzeichnungen des Malte Laurids Brigge*

The basic scheme of 'Atmen, du unsichtbares Gedicht', its rhythm of absorption of self into world, world into self, appears as a *programme* in Rilke's earliest verse:

> Vor lauter Lauschen und Staunen sei still,
> du mein tieftiefes Leben;
> daß du weißt, was der Wind dir will,
> eh noch die Birken beben.
>
> Und wenn dir einmal das Schweigen sprach,
> laß deine Sinne besiegen.
> Jedem Hauche gieb dich, gieb nach,
> er wird dich lieben und wiegen.
>
> Und dann meine Seele sei weit, sei weit,
> daß dir das Leben gelinge,
> breite dich wie ein Feierkleid
> über die sinnenden Dinge. (I,154)

'Leben', later a problematical term, is here merely reso-nantly imprecise, combining something of the sense of a personal life with the concept of an impersonal *élan vital* of the kind suggested in a contemporary poem:

> Du mußt das Leben nicht verstehen,
> dann wird es werden wie ein Fest. (I,153)

That the two meanings should be co-extensive - the personal life merged in the greater reality - is the underlying aspiration of the early *Mir zur Feier*. A quasi-oceanic

27

submission in the life of natural phenomena is balanced against an engulfing of those same phenomena in the 'breadth' of the soul, admission to this realm of circular benison being through 'lauter Lauschen und Staunen'. 'Lauschen' and its synonyms will remain positive terms in Rilke's vocabulary to the end, especially in the 'pure' sense of attentiveness to silence, to 'die ununterbrochene Nachricht, die aus Stille sich bildet'. But the ambiguous nature of visual perception is already in evidence in a collection whose predominant imagery is of darkness rather than daylight and clear contours. Certain poems suggest that the theme of darkness has deeper roots than those which cursory reading would attribute to such a well-worn fin-de-siècle motif:

> Denn manchmal bin ich vor dem Morgen bang
> und greife scheu nach seiner Rosen Röte - (I,195)

The contours of a world apprehended as menacing are blurred by the continuous evocation of darkness which also, through a paradoxical reversal of perception from the passive to the active mode, transforms anxiety into a sense of security:

> Aber die Abende sind mild und mein,
> von meinem Schauen sind sie still beschienen;
> in meinen Armen schlafen Wälder ein, -
> und ich bin selbst das Klingen über ihnen,
> und mit dem Dunkel in den Violinen
> verwandt durch all mein Dunkelsein.

The injunction of 'Vor lauter Lauschen' to enfold the world within the breadth of the soul is indeed obeyed, but only by an evasive nuancing of 'Staunen'.

One of the critics most sympathetic to Rilke's largely neglected early lyric work has written of its 'intuitive harmony', in which 'the self and the outer world...

continuously and automatically merged with one another'.[57]
The claim is in a sense that of the verse itself, but it
cannot be taken at face value; an impression of 'harmony'
is gained only by a liberal diffusion of sensibility in
bold extensions of the 'pathetic fallacy':

> Ich träumte, und mein Auge langte
> schon nach den blassen Sternen hin, -
> vom Dorfe her ein Ave bangte,
> und ein verlorner Falter schwankte
> im schneeig schimmernden Jasmin. (I,76)

Moreover, a marked characteristic of that sensibility, as
this example from the *Erste Gedichte* shows, is an insistent
but unfocussed sense of anxiety, belying any impression of
harmony. In the later and more self-conscious work of *Mir
zur Feier*, in which Rilke first gives direct expression to
that 'idealistic monism' which, as Frank Wood observes,
'Rilke retained, with variations, throughout his career',[58]
the anxiety is perceived as inimical to the celebration
promised by the title - the 'Fest' of intuitive harmony with
'life' - and is exorcized in a manoeuvre perhaps best described as a philosophical version of the 'pathetic fallacy':

> Und ich weiß jetzt: wie die Kinder werde.
> Alle Angst ist nur ein Anbeginn;
> aber ohne Ende ist die Erde,
> und das Bangen ist nur die Gebärde,
> und die Sehnsucht ist ihr Sinn - (I,155)

In the same way that the 'Dunkelsein' within reaches out to
a world of darkness, short-circuiting the menace involved in
'Staunen', so Rilke's persistent sense of anxiety is re-
interpreted as evidence of contact with the greater reality
of 'die Erde', and thus re-evaluated as a form of consolation.

One should not be deceived by the flaccidity of texture

of Rilke's earliest poems into reading them as merely re-
workings of conventional motifs. Beneath their surface one
senses deep-rooted anxieties, revealed principally in the
very strategies of nuance and paradox designed to contain or
exorcize them, to ensure that they do not check that determined urge towards celebration of harmony – an urge which,
as is increasingly evident in successive volumes, in fact
derives its main impetus *from* them.

The nature of these anxieties is more clearly, if still
on the whole inexplicitly, revealed in the next major collection. *Das Stundenbuch* is commonly considered the poetic
precipitate of Rilke's first Russian journey of 1899. But
any discontinuity between *Mir zur Feier* and *Die Gebete* (first
version of the later work) is more apparent than real. The
final poem of the earlier collection, though written at
Viareggio in 1898, would by no means seem out of place in
the later:

> Du darfst nicht warten, bis Gott zu dir geht
> und sagt: Ich bin.
> Ein Gott, der seine Stärke eingesteht,
> hat keinen Sinn.
> Da mußt du wissen, daß dich Gott durchweht
> seit Anbeginn,
> und wenn dein Herz dir glüht und nichts verrät,
> dann schafft er drin. (I,200)

Nor does this poem, though clearly introducing a new mode of
discourse – the quasi-theological – mark any radical departure in the collection in which it is placed. In the
loosely pantheistic context of *Mir zur Feier* it is but a
step from investing the natural world with the poet's own
yearnings, or claiming them to be the 'meaning' of Nature,
to attaching to them the attribute of divinity. The conception, most characteristic of *Das Buch vom mönchischen Leben*,
of a God totally immanent, ripening within the heart, can be

seen on close inspection as a particularly bold extension of
Rilke's already elaborated apparatus of exorcism.

In *Die Frühen Gedichte*, for instance, Rilke had written:

> Oft fühl ich in scheuen Schauern,
> wie tief ich im Leben bin.
> Die Worte sind nur die Mauern.
> Dahinter in immer blauern
> Bergen schimmert ihr Sinn. (I,193)

The image is taken up in the later collection; behind the
wall is now 'Nachbar Gott':

> Nur eine schmale Wand ist zwischen uns,
> durch Zufall; denn es könnte sein:
> ein Rufen deines oder meines Munds -
> und sie bricht ein
> ganz ohne Lärm und Laut. (I,255)

The 'Sinn' of reality has been brought close to hand, made
immediately available, because that meaning has been called
God, and God, neighbour; the empty resonance of 'Leben' and
'Erde' is merely replaced by the empty resonance of 'Gott'.
Empty, because just as earlier the world had been annexed as
cosmic extension of the self, now the world is infused with
the divine, and the divine claimed as an extension of the
self:

> Was wirst du tun, Gott, wenn ich sterbe?
> Ich bin dein Krug (wenn ich zerscherbe?)
> Ich bin dein Trank (wenn ich verderbe?)
> Bin dein Gewand und dein Gewerbe,
> mit mir verlierst du deinen Sinn. (I,275)

Again, the effect is to project on to a larger screen personal anxieties which are however neutralized by the con-
ferring of divinity on the screen. True, the poem concludes
with an explicit statement of anxiety:

                    Was wirst du tun, Gott? Ich bin bange.

But, as Eudo Mason has pointed out, the audacious theology
proposed by the monkish protagonist is enabled to acquire
'emotionally and imaginatively a certain pseudo-Christian
character' by the alternation of representations of God as
totally immanent with representations of a more traditional
kind, emphasizing the independent and overwhelming character
of the divine presence:[59]

          Du bist so groß, daß ich schon nicht mehr bin,
          wenn ich mich nur in deine Nähe stelle... (I,269)

The alternation not only assists suspension of disbelief on
the part of the reader; representations of God's transcendence, in the precarious and abstract series of equations
which sustains Rilke's pattern of relationships, exorcize
the anxieties woven into the representations of immanence.
If the ostensible theology of *Das Stundenbuch* makes the
'Sinn' of divinity dependent on the consciousness of the
monk/poet, it is no less true to say that the sense thus
conferred is made 'emotionally and imaginatively' possible
by the fact that it is on a divinity whose depiction
includes traditional elements that it is conferred.

    Furthermore, the 'diesseitig' concerns of the earlier
work are absorbed into rather than by-passed by the new mode
of discourse, as Käte Hamburger has recently emphasized.[60]
God is defined in *Das Stundenbuch* as 'der Dinge tiefer Ein-
begriff' (I,327), and the prevailing nocturnal imagery of
earlier collections persists in the conception of God as
'Dunkelheit', enfolding and reconciling 'Gestalten und
Flammen, Tiere und mich' (I,258). The collection opens
indeed with a summoning into the poet's presence of the perceived world, as bride to his perception:

                              32

Nichts war noch vollendet, eh ich es erschaut,
ein jedes Werden stand still.
Meine Blicke sind reif, und wie eine Braut
kommt jedem das Ding, das er will. (I,253)

The formulas echo the reversal of perceptual relationship
found in earlier work, and at the same time mirror, in their
general shape, the conception of God 'becoming' in the
poetic consciousness, thus disclosing the intimate connexion between the two levels of discourse. And in this
light, the alternation of transcendence and immanence in
representations of God receives another meaning, that defined by Käte Hamburger as 'die Haltung der Erkenntnis
und...nicht des Bekenntnisses'.[61] At this level, the alter-
nating pattern bears witness to an underlying tension; as
the same critic has shown, the collection is sustained
principally by two antithetical key-phrases - 'ich bin' and
'du bist' - and it is significant that the one excludes the
other. The rhythms of mutual absorption expressed as programme in 'Vor lauter Lauschen' and as experience in 'Atmen,
du unsichtbares Gedicht', appear here only in the two
extremes between which the collection moves. Affirmation of
the self is only possible through a reduction of the natural
world to abstract counters, the 'Dinge' which appear only as
components of the coruscating flow of imagery used by the
monk in addressing God - caught up, that is to say, in the
swirlings of poetic sensibility which is both monk and God.
The other side of the coin betrays why this should be so:
any direct experience of the world threatens to reduce the
self to a modality of perception, void of substance, as the
monk is reduced to the 'kleine Helle' which makes God's
darkness visible. From this vantage-point, one can readily
appreciate the mingled sense of aspiration and anxiety of
an earlier poem:

> Kann mir einer sagen, wohin
> ich mit meinem Leben reiche?
> Ob ich nicht auch noch im Sturme streiche
> und als Welle wohne im Teiche,
> und ob ich nicht selbst noch die blasse, bleiche
> frühlingfrierende Birke bin? (I,196)

Such ambiguous phrasings are generally the nearest that Rilke's early work comes towards admission of the threat contained in the ideal. It is noteworthy that the most explicit expression of a fear of dissolution in *Mir zur Feier* was excised from the revised version, no doubt precisely because it disturbed the even tenor of the work both emotionally and prosodically:

> Wenn einst, der alten Achsen
> entreift,
> die Nacht in wildem Weiterwachsen
> als blauer Brand aus allen Grenzen greift,
> und ich - in halbem Widerstreben - will,
> daß sie sich zu den letzten Welten wälze,
> und dabei still
> empfinde, wie ich schmelze...(III,259)

A similar formulation in *Das Buch vom mönchischen Leben* is displaced from the mouth of the major protagonist into that 'eines jungen Bruders':

> Ich verrinne, ich verrinne
> wie Sand, der durch Finger rinnt. (I,266)

Generally speaking, Rilke's work at this stage prefers to present aspiration as achievement, and to elaborate complex mechanisms for the neutralization of underlying anxieties. By the time of *Das Buch vom mönchischen Leben*, the mechanisms - nuancing of perceptual relationships, attribution of divinity to inchoate personal aspirations and anxieties, simultaneous expression and exorcism of a sense of threat by representations of divine transcendence - have become so

34

closely interwoven that only the extraordinary movement and
impetus of the collection, with its breathless exchange of
abstract counters - 'Leben', 'Gott', 'Dinge' - sustain the
balance.

Indeed, there is already a sense of breakdown in *Das
Buch von der Pilgerschaft*. The notion of pilgrimage is
itself a retreat from that of 'Nachbar Gott', and in the
opening poem of the collection, the 'Du' addressed is no
longer God, but the monk himself, from whom immediate experience of the divine has been withdrawn:

> Die große Einsamkeit beginnt,
> die Tage werden taub,
> aus deinen Sinnen nimmt der Wind
> die Welt wie welkes Laub. (I,305)

The second poem brings to the fore those anxieties
apparently exorcized in the earlier book:

> Ich war zerstreut; an Widersacher
> in Stücken war verteilt mein Ich.
> O Gott, mich lachten alle Lacher
> und alle Trinker tranken mich. (I,306)

Instead of reinforcing each other's existence, the three inhabitants of *Das Buch vom mönchischen Leben* - God, monk/poet
and natural world - are contrasted in mounting anxiety in a
later poem whose sense of a lack of reality in human life
calls into question the complacently idealistic experience
of earlier works:

> ...Keiner lebt sein Leben.
> Zufälle sind die Menschen... (I,316)

Rilke is unwilling to abandon the self-conscious monism
which formed the philosophical basis of that early experience -

> es ist ein großes Wunder in der Welt:
> ich fühle: *alles Leben wird gelebt* - (I,317)

and the search for the repository of this true life leads
him through a catalogue of winds, trees, flowers, animals
and birds to the anxious question:

> Wer lebt es denn? Lebst du es, Gott, - das Leben?

Desire is no longer taken for reality in the 'fremden
Stunde' of the later parts of *Das Stundenbuch*. If one can
speak of advance, it is in the maturer, more assured tone
which from time to time accompanies a more sharply delinea-
ted awareness of the gap between ideal and actuality:

> Wenn etwas mir vom Fenster fällt
> (und wenn es auch das Kleinste wäre)
> wie stürzt sich das Gesetz der Schwere
> gewaltig wie ein Wind vom Meere
> auf jeden Ball und jede Beere
> und trägt sie in den Kern der Welt...
> Nur wir, in unsrer Hoffahrt, drängen
> aus einigen Zusammenhängen
> in einer Freiheit leeren Raum,
> statt, klugen Kräften hingegeben,
> uns aufzuheben wie ein Baum. (I,320)

This contrast between the submission of natural objects and
human pride shows a more explicit awareness of the *price* of
that total absorption for which Rilke's early work had so
readily called, an awareness intensified in the introduction
of a motif which will be seen later as fraught with consequences for his major works - that of submission in death:

> Wir stehn in deinem Garten Jahr um Jahr
> und sind die Bäume, süßen Tod zu tragen;
> aber wir altern in den Erntetagen,
> und so wie Frauen, welche du geschlagen,
> sind wir verschlossen, schlecht und unfruchtbar.
> (I,348)

The motif receives its most positive statement in the ideal
figure, half St Francis, half new Messiah, whose idio-
syncratic apotheosis concludes the collection, and in whose
death human life bears fruit not only analogous to that of
the natural world, but accepted and absorbed into it:

> Und als er starb, so leicht wie ohne Namen,
> da war er ausgeteilt: sein Samen rann
> in Bächen, in den Bäumen sang sein Samen
> und sah ihn ruhig aus den Blumen an.
> Er lag und sang. (I,366)

In this conclusion, the motif is connected to a praise
of poverty, and of St Francis as 'der Armut großer Abend-
stern', which belong to a different order of discourse
altogether, and it will be nearly twenty years before a
similar apotheosis is celebrated for Orpheus. The concerns -
perhaps prematurely ambitious - of *Das Buch vom mönchischen
Leben* are already diluted in the remainder of *Das Stundenbuch*,
and disappear almost entirely in the various five-finger
exercises of *Das Buch der Bilder*, grouping poems written
over the years 1898 to 1906. Relevant in the present context
is only the regression, accompanied certainly by a general,
if uneven, advance in craftsmanship, to the impressionistic
vision and autumnal melancholy of *Die Frühen Gedichte*, and
the occasional expression of a sense of imprisonment within
sensibility, an unfulfilled longing for a reality 'out
there':

> Ich möchte aus meinem Herzen hinaus
> unter den großen Himmel treten.
> Ich möchte beten.
> Und einer wirklich von allen Sternen
> müßte wirklich noch sein. (I,397)

*   *   *   *   *   *   *   *

From the careful separation of poems between *Larenopfer*,
written entirely in 1895, and *Traumgekrönt*, spanning the

37

years 1894 to 1896; through the intercalation of *Das Buch von der Armut und vom Tode* into the gathering of material for *Das Buch der Bilder*; to the extraordinary overlapping of *Duineser Elegien* and *Sonette an Orpheus*, Rilke acknowledged the differing strengths and directions of his winds of inspiration, and safeguarded the homogeneity of individual collections from the vagaries of mere chronology. It is thus all the more interesting that in adding some thirty poems to the second edition of *Das Buch der Bilder* in 1906, he reserved four poems for the later *Neue Gedichte*. Of these, 'Der Panther' was seen by Rilke himself as first-fruit of the discipline 'imposed' by Rodin. The remaining three - 'Hetären-Gräber', 'Geburt der Venus' and 'Orpheus. Eurydike. Hermes' - may have been grouped together simply in terms of thematic source, but it seems likely that Rilke transferred them to the *Neue Gedichte*, not so much because they showed any formal affinity with 'Der Panther', but because he sensed in them an *ambitiousness* foreign to the general tonality of the earlier collection. 'Orpheus. Eurydike. Hermes' is particularly interesting in this respect; it leads directly out of the conclusion of *Das Buch von der Armut und vom Tode*, foreshadows many features of major poems of the *Neue Gedichte*, and points beyond them into the elegiac years, thus forming a striking link between the early and the mature Rilke.

Orpheus appears first:

Voran der schlanke Mann im blauen Mantel,
der stumm und ungeduldig vor sich aussah.
Ohne zu kauen fraß sein Schritt den Weg
in großen Bissen...
Und seine Sinne waren wie entzweit:
indes der Blick ihm wie ein Hund vorauslief,
umkehrte, kam und immer wieder weit
und wartend an der nächsten Wendung stand, -
blieb sein Gehör wie ein Geruch zurück. (I,543)

The description takes up the condemnation of human

impatience contrasted, in *Das Buch von der Armut und vom Tode*, with the submissiveness of natural objects. The description of Eurydice, on the other hand, derives from the apotheosis of St Francis:

> Sie war schon aufgelöst wie langes Haar
> und hingegeben wie gefallner Regen
> und ausgeteilt wie hundertfacher Vorrat.
>
> Sie war schon Wurzel.

'Wurzel' picks up the opening threads of the poem, with the notion of the dead feeding the living:

> Das war der Seelen wunderliches Bergwerk.
> Wie stille Silbererze gingen sie
> als Adern durch sein Dunkel. Zwischen Wurzeln
> entsprang das Blut, das fortgeht zu den Menschen...

Submission, in the form of being 'ausgelöst', 'hingegeben', brings a fruitfulness - a transformation into 'Vorrat' - denied to those excoriated in *Das Buch von der Armut und vom Tode* as 'verschlossen, schlecht und unfruchtbar'.

And yet Eurydice herself is precisely 'verschlossen'; in paradoxical association with her 'Aufgelöstheit', and contrasting in a different mode with Orpheus's impatience, she exhibits also a sense of closed self-containment:

> Sie war in sich. Und ihr Gestorbensein
> erfüllte sie wie Fülle.
> Wie eine Frucht von Süßigkeit und Dunkel,
> so war sie voll vom ihrem großen Tode,
> der also neu war, daß sie nichts begriff.
>
> Sie war in einem neuen Mädchentum
> und unberührbar; ihr Geschlecht war zu
> wie eine junge Blume gegen Abend...

This quality too, like its apparent antithesis, is closely woven together with the theme of death; it is precisely her

'Gestorbensein', Rilke insists, with its withdrawal from
human intercourse, which sustains her self-containment:

> und ihre Hände waren der Vermählung
> so sehr entwöhnt, daß selbst des leichten Gottes
> unendlich leise, leitende Berührung
> sie kränkte wie zu sehr Vertraulichkeit.

Totally contained, and yet endlessly given out - the paradox
is sustained only by the image of death. To a still greater
extent than in the St Francis poem, this configuration will
be fraught with consequences for Rilke's later work.

Eurydice's 'Aufgelöstheit' answers to the primary
impulse of Rilke's early poetry - to experience the transcendental and the phenomenal, the self and the world, as
continuous. Her self-containment foreshadows the almost
wilfully discontinuous world of the *Neue Gedichte*, composed
of objects sharply-contoured and self-sufficient, isolated
gestures and situations with no interplay, for which the
panther's 'Tanz von Kraft um eine Mitte' stands as early
paradigm. Just as Eurydice shrinks from Hermes's touch, so
a similar, though often more loftily indifferent attitude
of *noli me tangere* unites the most disparate inhabitants of
this world. Parrots preen themselves preciously; flamingoes
narcissistically nurse their beauty and, if disturbed by
envious shrieks, 'schreiten einzeln ins Imaginäre' (I,630).
In the transcendental mode, Buddha is

> Mitte aller Mitten, Kern der Kerne,
> Mandel, die sich einschließt und versüßt (I,642)

and disdains mere mortality:

> O er ist Alles. Wirklich, warten wir,
> daß er uns sähe? Sollte er bedürfen?
> Und wenn wir hier uns vor ihm niederwürfen,
> er bliebe tief und träge wie ein Tier. (I,496)

A direct line links Eurydice's 'neues Mädchentum' and the
angelic self-sufficiency of the Elegies; the fundamental
import of the image will be examined shortly.

One of the finest of these explorations of self-
containment, and one which, moreover, probes the poet's
stance before a world apprehended in the mode of discontinuity, is 'Die Gazelle'. From the outset the emphasis
is not on simple description, but on the act of perception,
and on the tension implicit in the poet's quest to render
in words the almost magical *separateness* of the animal:

> Verzauberte: wie kann der Einklang zweier
> erwählter Worte je den Reim erreichen,
> der in dir kommt und geht (I,506)

The poem then continues as if in the descriptive manner, but
the 'Laub und Leier' evoked are only partially visual,
awakening associations to be explored later, and the second
stanza commences on an arabesque of similes which take the
reader apparently far away from the object of description:

> Aus deiner Stirne steigen Laub und Leier,
>
> und alles Deine geht schon im Vergleich
> durch Liebeslieder, deren Worte, weich
> wie Rosenblätter, dem, der nicht mehr liest,
> sich auf die Augen legen, die er schließt...

The connexions are deliberately tenuous, while reinforcing
the impression of delicacy which is the ostensible purpose
of the simile. But at the same time as the images seem to
move away from the animal itself, a subtle process is set
in motion which takes one back, via the hypothetical reader
of love-songs, to the situation of poet gazing at animal.
And with the third stanza the poem returns suddenly and at
first sight unexpectedly to direct address:

41

um dich zu sehen...

The reader closing his eyes to the words of the book, only
to find them pressing gently on his eyes, merges with the
poet closing his eyes to the gazelle - to see it the better.
Initially addressed as 'Verzauberte', the animal is transposed into an inner world, and yet it is out of this inner
vision that there arises an arrestingly visual image:

> ...hingetragen, als
> wäre mit Sprüngen jeder Lauf geladen
> und schösse nur nicht ab, solang der Hals
> das Haupt ins Horchen hält...

The final image seems at first sight totally gratuitous:

> ...wie wenn beim Baden
> im Wald die Badende sich unterbricht:
> den Waldsee im gewendeten Gesicht.

In fact, it is far from gratuitous, though it is part of the
poem's strategy that it should appear so. Firstly, it
brings together the qualities of delicacy explored in the
second quatrain and of poise explored in the first tercet.
Secondly, the introduction of the wood echoes the 'Laub und
Leier' of the first quatrain, whilst the evocation of 'Diane
aux bains' reinforces the intimation of the mythical figure
of Apollo in 'Leier', thus relating the inner world in which
the animal moves to realms of legend and art. Thirdly, this
magic realm is pictured in the sequestered woodland lake, the
gazelle's self-absorption in the absorption of the bather in
her reflection in the lake; and these associations in turn
suggest another - between Acteon interrupting Diana and poet
interrupting gazelle. Which brings the poem back to its
starting-point - the poet's feeling of presumption in
attempting to capture in words the self-contained, quasi-
magical being of the animal. And yet the opening question
has been answered by the poem; by a detour which proved
strategic, the web of associations has evoked those very

42

qualities which seemed to forbid the attempt.

'Die Gazelle' is a bravura performance, both playful
and with an underlying seriousness, of one of a number of
models of transformation with which the *Neue Gedichte* are
concerned. To enter into any prolonged discussion of those
models - the transformation of time into space, of movement
into stasis, of reality into reflection - would be beyond
the present purpose, which is to enquire into the
existential roots of this aesthetic. 'Self-containment',
in the volumes as a whole as in 'Die Gazelle', is both
starting-point - the mode of apprehension of the world under
the strict painterly discipline of these years - and end-
product - the 'Kunstding' in its self-sufficiency, its
umbilical cord with the 'Klage' which gave it birth
apparently cut and disposed of. But certain poems remind
the reader of the source of Rilke's fascination with the
image of self-containment, its function as implicit contrast
with the limitations and contingencies of human life and
consciousness. Such a poem is 'Die Rosenschale', placed
strategically at the end of the first volume.

The opening of the poem takes one back to the Orpheus
of the 1904 poem:

> Zornige sahst du flackern, sahst zwei Knaben
> zu einem Etwas sich zusammenballen,
> das Haß war und sich auf der Erde wälzte
> wie ein von Bienen überfallnes Tier;
> Schauspieler, aufgetürmte Übertreiber,
> rasende Pferde, die zusammenbrachen,
> den Blick wegwerfend, bläkend das Gebiß
> als schälte sich der Schädel aus dem Maule. (I,552)

The image of human life thus presented is the obverse of the
combination of qualities which make up the gazelle - a
parody of self-containment in the rolling together of the

boys into a mass that composes only hatred, a histrionic
exaggeration at the opposite pole from poise. Against this
picture is set the bowl of roses,

>   die unvergeßlich ist und angefüllt
>   mit jenem Äußersten von Sein und Neigen,
>   Hinhalten, Niemals-Gebenkönnen, Dastehn...

And yet the contrast is not simply elegiac, for those
qualities are at least potentially, and in a sense which
the poem will unfold, human:

>   ...das unser sein mag: Äußerstes auch uns.

The delineation of the roses as

>   Lautloses Leben, Aufgehn ohne Ende,
>   Raum-brauchen ohne Raum von jenem Raum
>   zu nehmen, den die Dinge rings verringern

is less description than designation of ontological *status*.
Visual perception - the observation that the opening-up of
roses is a kind of 'Aufgehn' which utilizes no extra space
- passes over into another dimension, as the phenomenal context gives way to a purely mental space akin to the magical
realm of the gazelle:

>   fast nicht Umrissen-sein wie Ausgespartes
>   und lauter Inneres...

Dissolution of contour melts away the potential tension of
visual perception, leaving the roses 'vorhanden' - present,
and, for all their self-containment, available. The poise
of the gazelle and the energy of the panther are intimately
combined in the description of the closed petals:

>   Und dies: daß eins sich aufschlägt wie ein Lid,
>   und drunten liegen lauter Augenlider,
>   geschlossene, als ob sie, zehnfach schlafend,
>   zu dämpfen hätten eines Innern Sehkraft.

But where the panther's gaze is passive, that of the roses
is actively at work, filtering darkness out of light and
creating gestures which, though imperceptible in themselves,
send rays streaming out into the cosmos:

> Gebärden von so kleinem Ausschlagswinkel,
> daß sie unsichtbar blieben, liefen ihre
> Strahlen nicht auseinander in das Weltall.

The contrast with the histrionic, self-destructive energy of
the opening, and the link with Eurydice, is completed by the
interpretation of the opening and loss of petals as a form
of *submission*:

> Und *was* sie abtun, wie das leicht und schwer,
> wie es ein Mantel, eine Last, ein Flügel
> und eine Maske sein kann, je nach dem,
> und *wie* sie's abtun: wie vor dem Geliebten.

This playfully anthropomorphic development is intensified with an air of breathless delight into an explosion of
images, from the domesticity of a warm vest to the delicacy
of a china cup, but then leads unexpectedly to the bare
conclusion:

> und jene da, die nichts enthält als sich.

Such bareness is however the springboard for the final triumph, for that simple self-containment is a containment of
the whole of reality:

> Und sind nicht alle so, nur sich enthaltend,
> wenn Sich-enthalten heißt: die Welt da draußen
> und Wind und Regen und Geduld des Frühlings
> und Schuld und Unruh und vermummtes Schicksal
> und Dunkelheit der abendlichen Erde
> bis auf der Wolken Wandel, Flucht und Anflug,
> bis auf den vagen Einfluß ferner Sterne
> in eine Hand voll Innres zu verwandeln.

> Nun liegt es sorglos in den offnen Rosen.

These qualities - active, transforming energy combined with
total submission, a self-containment which is yet containment of the cosmos - are not ours. But they may be 'ours',
as the second stanza tentatively suggested. For the transformation of cosmos into 'Inneres' in the roses is
paralleled by, indeed is indistinguishable from, the transformation of roses from mere phenomena to mental space. The
double movement asserts the possibility of appropriating
poetically the qualities whose lack in actual human life
forms the elegiac background to the poem.

It is hardly likely that the placing of 'Die Rosenschale' at the conclusion of the first and more important
part of the *Neue Gedichte* was fortuitous - nor the placing
of 'Archaïscher Torso Apollos' at the opening of the second
part. The latter poem subtly alters, however, the balance
of elegy and triumph, while sharing many features with the
poems already discussed. Its turning away from the merely
visual is abrupt:

> Wir kannten nicht sein unerhörtes Haupt,
> darin die Augenäpfel reiften... (I,557)

But this negation only serves to emphasize the strength of
what is visible:

> ...Aber
> sein Torso glüht noch wie ein Kandelaber,
> in dem sein Schauen, nur zurückgeschraubt,
> sich hält und glänzt.

The rose's 'Innern Sehkraft' is intensified from bold metaphor to paradox, while the unashamed delight of 'Die Rosenschale' is modified to a mood of cautious appraisal echoed
in the conditional mood:

> ...Sonst könnte nicht der Bug
> der Brust dich blenden, und im leisen Drehen
> der Lenden könnte nicht ein Lächeln gehen
> zu jener Mitte, die die Zeugung trug.

The implications of poised self-containment in 'sich hält
und glänzt' are reinforced by the image of the smile, while
the paradox of the torso's 'Schauen' is taken up in the
poet's mounting awareness of his own gaze being answered by
the contrary activity of the statue:

> Sonst stünde dieser Stein entstellt und kurz
> unter der Schultern durchsichtigem Sturz
> und flimmerte nicht so wie Raubtierfelle;
>
> und bräche nicht aus allen seinen Rändern
> aus wie ein Stern...

The 'breaking-out' of the stone marks also the breaking-out
of the torso's accumulated energy into the movement of the
poem, which moves decisively back into the indicative:

> ...denn da ist keine Stelle
> die dich nicht sieht.

The whole poem has been built on a series of paradoxes, of
which the double negative of the conclusion is a formal
echo. That the headless torso should exhibit a poised
self-containment akin to that of the perfectly-formed
gazelle; that, deprived of eyes, it should yet possess a
power of sight which overwhelms the gaze of the poet -
these prepare the way for the final paradox that contempla-
tion of an antique statue should issue forth in a present-
tense moral imperative:

> ...du mußt dein Leben ändern.

Yet this paradox is of a different order from those
which precede it. Written towards the end of the period of

composition of *Neue Gedichte*, 'Archaïscher Torso Apollos'
contrasts their world with the imperfections of human life.
Its final paradox undermines the series of paradoxes on
which the collection so heavily depends, revealing them as
mechanisms of transcendence of underlying anxieties, likely
to be nullified by a reversal such as that which concludes
the torso-poem, or that suffered by the goldsmith of 'Der
Reliquienschrein', forced to his knees by the shrine he has
himself created:

> der ihn zu gewahren schien
> und ihn, plötzlich um sein Dasein fragend,
> ansah wie aus Dynastien.(I,578)

The only triumph accorded to Orpheus in 'Orpheus.
Eurydike. Hermes' is his creation of a world of song,

> ...in der
> alles noch einmal da war: Wald und Tal
> und Weg und Ortschaft, Feld und Fluß und Tier...

Such triumph is not sufficient for him; he seeks the more
directly existential goal of Eurydice's return to earth, a
prize denied him for his lack of Eurydice's own qualities.
Rilke sustains, in the *Neue Gedichte*, the renunciation from
which Orpheus lapses. Indeed, he does not even so much
create, like Orpheus before his lapse, 'eine Welt aus
Klage'; the world of the *Neue Gedichte*, like the inverted
world of the 1906 poem, is an obverse world. It is possible,
that is to say - abstracting for a moment the very real
poetic triumphs of the volumes - to read them in negative,
each quality celebrated pointing to the anxiety, the 'Klage',
which gives force to the quality. 'Archaïscher Torso
Apollos' and 'Die Rosenschale', though the earlier moves
from anxiety to celebration, and the later points only
implicitly to anxiety, both illustrate the extent to which

anxieties remain the essential dynamic of Rilke's work, and
renunciation of the existential perspective would not be
sustained beyond the ebbing of that particular tide of
inspiration. One of the most characteristic features of
Rilke's career is a relentless raising of the stakes, each
temporary point of balance being sooner or later overtaken
by more radical doubts, and in this respect 'Die Rosenschale', paradigm of the systems of transformation which
underpin the *Neue Gedichte*, represents a point of balance no
more secure, if vastly more achieved, than that of *Das Buch
vom mönchischen Leben*. Indeed, the pattern characterizing
the earlier period - the elaboration of a complex strategy
for the transcendence of anxiety, itself revealed only by
implication, followed by a regression to a more direct
encounter - is repeated in the middle years, insofar as
completion of the second volume of the *Neue Gedichte* was
followed by the elaboration of the long-harboured fragments
of *Die Aufzeichnungen des Malte Laurids Brigge* into the most
painfully explicit treatment of existential doubts and fears.

*   *   *   *   *   *   *   *

Malte introduces himself. A young man of twenty-eight,
he is author of a study of Carpaccio which he now repudiates,
of a drama which seems to him false and ambiguous, and of a
number of verses. Of the verses he has this to say:

> Ach, aber mit Versen ist so wenig getan, wenn man sie
> früh schreibt. Man sollte warten damit und Sinn und
> Süßigkeit sammeln ein ganzes Leben lang und ein langes
> womöglich, und dann, ganz zum Schluß, vielleicht könnte
> man dann zehn Zeilen schreiben, die gut sind. Denn
> Verse sind nicht, wie die Leute meinen, Gefühle (die
> hat man früh genug), - es sind Erfahrungen. (VI,723)

The distinction between 'Gefühle' and 'Erfahrungen' strikes
a personal note, and not only because Rilke had once
attempted to launch a new poetic movement under the title of

49

'Gefühlslyrik'. There is no reason to suppose that poetry must of necessity be such as Malte claims, but the comment acquires force in the context of Rilke's early verse which habitually presented as the fruit of long experience the barely articulate aspiration of personal sensibility. To this extent, Malte's words are a clear abjuration of all his work before his arrival in Paris. But the terms in which he continues do not suggest a defence of the *Neue Gedichte*. Certainly, the initial stress is placed on the necessity of an encounter with the world about the poet - 'Um eines Verses willen muß man viele Städte sehen, Menschen und Dinge' (VI.724) - but in the development of this theme the isolated, contoured evocations of the *Neue Gedichte* are rapidly superseded in a lyrical evocation of meetings and departures, days of meditation, nights of love and nights of travel, the labours of childbirth and the hour of death - and of *childhood* experience. Eudo Mason has pointed out how, in comparing his two 'Masters' of this period, Rilke linked Jacobsen with childhood, Rodin with maturity;[62] in this respect the *Aufzeichnungen* were written under the sign of Jacobsen. And the theme of childhood is that of a task still to be performed - 'Auch die Kindheit würde also gewissermaßen noch zu leisten sein' (VI,856) - suggesting a feeling that the renunciation of a directly existential perspective in the *Neue Gedichte* had proved impossible to sustain, their 'maturity' premature.

Moreover, poetry, in Malte's programme, is not to arise directly from these experiences, nor even from their recollection in tranquillity, but only out of the moment 'wenn sie Blut werden in uns, Blick und Gebärde, namenlos und nicht mehr zu unterscheiden von uns selbst' (VI, 725). On such criteria, Rilke, like Malte, could well conclude that 'alle meine Verse ...sind anders entstanden, also sind es keine' (VI,725). Indeed, to encounter reality at the

requisite depth, Malte suggests, is a task which has so far
eluded not only him, but the whole of humanity. A little
further on, he speaks of Nature as 'immer bemüht...von
ihren tiefsten Geheimnissen die Aufmerksamkeit der Menschen
abzulenken' (VI,725), and his meditation concludes:

> Ist es möglich, daß man trotz Erfindungen und
> Fortschritten, trotz Kultur, Religion und Welt-
> Weisheit an der Oberfläche des Lebens geblieben
> ist?...
> Ja, es ist möglich. (VI,727)

Aware of the enormity of the task, Malte is yet convinced
that he, 'dieses Nichts', 'dieser junge, belanglose Ausländer', must take it on.

The task begins with *seeing*. 'Ich lerne sehen', Malte
reports to himself (VI,710). 'Habe ich es schon gesagt?
Ich lerne sehen' (VI,711). However insignificant the
object, the evidence of his experience is to be water-tight,
defensible before an imaginary judge as being not just the
truth, but the whole truth:

> Habe ich schon gesagt, daß er blind war? Nein?
> Also er war blind. Er war blind und schrie. Ich
> fälsche, wenn ich das sage, ich unterschlage den
> Wagen, den er schob, ich tue, als hätte ich nicht
> bemerkt, daß er Blumenkohl ausrief...Ich habe einen
> alten Mann gesehen, der blind war und schrie. Das
> habe ich gesehen. Gesehen. (VI,748)

Neither the lyrical evocation of 'Erfahrungen' in Malte's
programme, nor the Parnassian exotica of *Neue Gedichte* prepare one for the results of this refusal of selectivity.
The notation of the seen commences in the third sentence of
the work with the grimmest aspects of city life - 'Ich habe
gesehen: Hospitäler. Ich habe einen Menschen gesehen,
welcher schwankte und umsank' (VI,709). Flamingos and rose-

bowls give way to trams and beggars; nights of love to
nights of insomnia with meaningless snatches of conversation
heard through the open window. In a letter to an unnamed
friend, Malte reformulates his programme, not in terms of
distant ideals, but in terms of the necessary, and already
sufficiently overwhelming preliminary task, that of *accepting*, as Baudelaire in *Une Charogne* accepts, the reality of
even the most loathsome of experiences:

> Was sollte er tun, da ihm das widerfuhr? Es war seine
> Aufgabe, in diesem Schrecklichen, scheinbar nur
> Widerwärtigen das Seiende zu sehen, das unter allem
> Seienden gilt. Auswahl und Ablehnung giebt es nicht.
> (VI,775)

In the private meditation which follows the brave hopes
of the letter, however, Malte begins to realize that he
follows through this resolution at the cost of his own
existence. For the poise and detachment of Baudelaire's
calculated 'realism' is totally foreign to Malte. In the
opening pages of the novel, an ironic, even slightly dandy-
ish tone preserves a certain distance between narrator and
events - 'Zwei Francs für die Sterbestunde', 'Natürlich
fabrikmäßig' (VI,713) - but it cannot be sustained. After
only three weeks in Paris, Malte feels himself so much
changed by his experiences that he can no longer write to
his erstwhile friends, feeling himself a different person
from the one they knew. And this change is precisely a
result of his seeing:

> Ich lerne sehen. Ich weiß nicht, woran es liegt, es
> geht alles tiefer in mich ein und bleibt nicht an der
> Stelle stehen, wo es sonst immer zu Ende war. Ich
> habe ein Inneres, von dem ich nicht wußte. Alles
> geht jetzt dorthin. Ich weiß nicht, was dort
> geschieht. (VI,710f.)

'Was dort geschieht' is rapidly revealed. Sitting in the

Bibliothèque Nationale, Malte congratulates himself on his privileges - 'was für ein Schicksal, ich, vielleicht der armsäligste von diesen Lesenden, ein Ausländer: ich habe einen Dichter' (VI,742). But his self-conscious defence of his own status, marked by his clothes - clean, if a little shabby - is soon undermined:

> Aber es giebt doch ein paar Existenzen, auf dem Boulevard Saint-Michel zum Beispiel, und in der rue Racine, die lassen sich nicht irremachen, die pfeifen auf die Gelenke. Die sehen mich an und wissen es. Die wissen, daß ich eigentlich zu ihnen gehöre, daß ich nur ein bißchen Komödie spiele. (VI,742)

He sits in a 'crémerie', and finds himself next to a dying man. Back in his room, he assures himself that nothing has happened - 'und doch habe ich jenen Mann nur begreifen können, weil auch in mir etwas vor sich geht, das anfängt, mich von allem zu entfernen und abzutrennen' (VI,755). He stands long before the crumbling inner wall of a demolished house, and the picture is imprinted on his mind, he insists, by the shock of recognition - 'Ich erkenne das alles hier, und darum geht es so ohne weiteres in mich ein: es ist zu Hause in mir' (VI,751). Fever brings back the anxieties of childhood, experienced now without the saving presence of the mother, and shorn of the particularities which enable them to be rationalized, so that they now form only 'das Große', unnamed and overwhelming. Recovery and an attempt to return to the security of the library only precipitate Malte's collapse: following a St Vitus's victim along the Boulevard Saint-Michel, he is 'bound', despite himself, to the victim's strenuous attempts to escape attention, and when Malte finally loses sight of him, he feels emptied, not just of strength, but of *self*:

> Was hätte es für einen Sinn gehabt, noch irgendwohin zu gehen, ich war leer. Wie ein leeres Papier trieb ich an den Häusern entlang, den Boulevard wieder hinauf.
> (VI,774)

The boundaries between inner and outer crumble, but not in favour of the 'Fest' promised by Rilke's early idealism; all the 'Qual und Grauen' without serve as catalyst to release 'das Große' within, and the self *disintegrates*:

> Wie ein Käfer, auf den man tritt, so quillst du aus
> dir hinaus, und dein bißchen obere Härte und Anpassung
> ist ohne Sinn. (VI,777)

'Der Arzt hat mich nicht verstanden', complains Malte (VI,758). Rilke himself felt that Freud would have understood him too well, and in explaining his condition, would have unwound the springs of his creativity. But from the critic's point of view, though 'Erklären', in Dilthey's sense, is at best irrelevant, at worst an impertinence, 'Verstehen' is precisely the goal of literary study, and *Malte*, though in some sense it interprets Rilke's other, especially his earlier, texts, itself requires interpretation. An interpretation which identifies protagonist and author too simplistically, and then sees the behaviour of the author/protagonist as evidence of a condition to be uncovered and translated without residue into its aetiology, may be ruled out. But an existential psychology which sees such behaviour as a language and a strategy for survival in a condition different only in degree from 'normality', may be of help, insofar as it comes close to Rilke's own attempt, in creating the 'anti-self' of Malte, to embody in intensified form and thus hopefully exorcize anxieties by no means confined to the clinically psychotic. R.D. Laing's characterization of the schizoid experience as a basic ontological insecurity, giving rise to anxieties concerning the substantiality of the self and its ability to sustain relationships with the world of experience and with other subjectivities, is such an attempt, and may provide a basic *language* for the analysis of Malte's anxieties. The primary anxiety, in Laing's analysis, is for the identity and

54

autonomy of the self, appearing in two major forms. One is
the fear of 'implosion', regarded as a basic reaction to the
world of experience, the 'terror of the experience of the
world as liable at any moment to crash in and obliterate all
identity as a gas will rush in and obliterate a vacuum',
with the result that 'the individual feels that, like the
vacuum, he is empty'.[63] A secondary phenomenon allied to
this primary anxiety and capable of being elaborated into a
defence, is that of disembodiment, or detachment from one's
own embodied self; in this perspective, the body is felt 'as
the core of a false self, which a detached, disembodied,
"inner", "true" self looks on at'.[64] The second major form
of anxiety, experienced in relation to other subjectivities,
is a fear of 'engulfment'; Laing's characterization of this
anxiety is, worth quoting at length:

> In this the individual dreads relatedness as such, with
> anyone or anything, or indeed, even with himself, be-
> cause his uncertainty about the stability of his auto-
> nomy lays him open to the dread lest in any relation-
> ship he will lose his autonomy and identity...Engulf-
> ment is felt as being a risk in being understood (thus
> grasped, comprehended), in being loved, or even simply
> in being seen. To be hated may be feared for other
> reasons, but to be hated as such is often less disturb-
> ing than to be destroyed, as it is felt, through being
> engulfed by love.[65]

That such analyses were in some sense understood by
Rilke himself is evident from the pages of *Malte Laurids
Brigge*. The gradual disintegration of Malte's 'bißchen
obere Härte' to the point of 'implosion' has already been
charted; the return to childhood experiences, already
broached and continued in more detail after this first
climactic point, echoes - or, in terms of Malte's own biography, prefigures - the Paris experiences. It would no
doubt be unwise to interpret the various incidents related
in too directly behavioural a manner; much of this material

is purely 'literary' in form, to be seen either as building
up a generalized picture of 'das Unheimliche', or as
symbolic expressions of what Rilke would later call 'die
ewige Strömung...durch beide Bereiche', the fundamental
unity of life and death – itself an already intellectualized
concept, symbolic rather than existential in import. But a
general anxiety concerning the identity of the self is
constantly in evidence, and one episode, that concerning the
mirror, is especially explicit. At first, Malte's dressing-
up before the mirror is a triumphant procession of 'false
selves' which mask anxieties concerning the autonomy of the
'inner self':

> Diese Verstellungen gingen indessen nie so weit, daß
> ich mich mir selber entfremdet fühlte; im Gegenteil,
> je vielfältiger ich mich abwandelte, desto überzeugter
> wurde ich von mir selbst. (VI,804)

But a trivial disturbance destroys the child's delight, and
when he then looks back at the mirror, not voluntarily, but
with a sense of dread and compulsion, reality seems to have
passed totally out of his 'inner self' into the 'false self'
embodied in the dressed-up figure. The result is an
'implosion' in which the vacuum of the self is taken over
by the now substantialized figure:

> Aber in demselben Moment, da ich dies dachte, geschah
> das Äußerste: ich verlor allen Sinn, ich fiel einfach
> aus. Eine Sekunde lang hatte ich eine unbeschreib-
> liche, wehe und vergebliche Sehnsucht nach mir, dann
> war nur noch er: es war nichts außer ihm. (VI,808)

Malte's dual situation of protagonist and narrator
complicates the interpretation of his relationships with
others. As narrator, he uses others frequently as 'Vokabeln
seiner Not', images of his own anxieties. Such is the case
with the woman in rue Notre-Dame des Champs, whose 'Nicht-
gesicht' Malte fears to look upon; with the various Parisian

outcasts, 'Speichel des Schicksals', with whom he has a
frightening intuition of brotherhood; with the patients in
the Salpêtrière, whose identity is symbolically extinguished
by the bandages signifying the illnesses which have invaded
them and destroyed their autonomy. Most of all it is the
case with the dying and dead who fill the pages of the
novel. For it is not the cessation of life which holds
Malte's horrified attention so much as the extinction of
personal identity. The novel opens with the words: 'So,
also hierher kommen die Leute, um zu leben, ich würde eher
meinen, es stürbe sich hier' (VI,709), the impersonal construction adumbrating the notion of mass-produced death,
developed a few pages later into a scathing indictment of
the anonymity of life and death in the modern city -
'Voilà votre mort, Monsieur'. The contrast of this form of
death with the death of the old Chamberlain at Ulsgaard,
who dies his own princely death, is presented as a contrast
of a cultural-historical order, but by no means all the
deaths remembered from Malte's childhood support the
implicit assertion. The horror of his mother's death is
conveyed in the impersonal indifference of an adverb: 'Und
Maman starb indessen' (VI,811). Christian Brahe is not
even known to be dead, but his extinction as an identity is
graphically evoked in the supposition that he and his servant exist now only 'auf der Schiffsliste eines ver-
schollenen Schiffes unter Namen, die nicht die ihren waren'
(VI,812). Erik Brahe's death represents the collapse of a
known personality into the conjectures of imaginary visitors
looking at his picture in the gallery - 'Dieser Knabe ist
als Knabe gestorben, gleichviel wann' (VI,819). Malte's
grandmother's death is a slow extinction of sense, so that
the death of her body comes as an irrelevant, almost
unnoticed accident - 'Sophie Oxe, deren Tür offenstand,
hatte nichts gehört. Da man sie am Morgen fand, war sie
kalt wie Glas' (VI,823). The death of Malte's father

occurs in his absence, but is nonetheless the most extensively
treated: in particular, the slip of paper found in his wallet,
telling of Christian IV's death, serves as device for general-
izing a view of death as an overwhelming of the individual by
an outside force. Only one word - that is, only one, completely
unindividualized experience - remains in the hour of death, 'das
einzige, das es noch gab' (VI,858). The directness of the link
between Malte's fear of death and the existential anxieties he
suffers as living person is most explicitly revealed in the
encounter with the dying man in the 'crêmerie'. He awaits death,
Malte surmises, as an invasion against which he no longer defends
himself. 'Und ich wehre mich noch.', Malte continues (VI,755);
the invasion of 'das Große' is an ever-present threat in life,
and merely sealed in death.

Malte's reaction as *protagonist* to others is marked by a
fear of engulfment, bearing witness from a different perspective
to the same fundamental ontological insecurity. From one point
of view, the outcasts of Paris offer an externalized form of
Malte's fears of self-alienation, and in this perspective they
appear as brothers, though menacingly so. Later, however, the
relationship is re-evaluated; as Malte becomes more aware of
the emptiness within him, the sheer substantiality of the
beggars becomes a cause of envy:

> Nein, es ist nicht, daß ich mich von ihnen
> unterscheiden will; aber ich überhübe mich,
> wollte ich ihnen gleich sein. Ich bin es
> nicht. Ich hätte weder ihre Stärke noch ihr Maß.(VI,903f.)

Despite their invisibility, and even their possibly imaginary
nature, neighbours are lent this extra dimension of substantiality in contrast to Malte's own sense of unreality. This contrast is felt as a form of threat, so that to tell of his
neighbours would be to tell of the 'Krankheitserscheinungen, die
sie in mir gezeugt haben' (VI,864). The hostility of others is

assumed, axiomatic; Malte decides that he should not waste his
strength on keeping the stove alight, for 'wenn ich dann unter
die Leute komme, haben sie es natürlich leicht' (VI,753). He
feels secure in the library not because of the friendly relationships he entertains with the other readers, but because of the
lack of any relationship at all: 'Warum sind sie nicht immer so?
Du kannst hingehen zu einem und ihn leise anrühen: er fühlt
nichts'(VI,741).

It is however in the strategies developed to cope with
insecurity of this order that the insecurity is most fully
revealed. Laing defines two principal strategies, the first
being simply isolation, avoidance of the threat posed by
others. The second is the cultivation of an inner life
detached from the outer self of action, the inner self being
felt to be 'ungraspable, elusive, transcendent'. Fearing to
be comprehended through his actions, the insecure person
associates action with a false self, while '"he", his "self"
is endless possibility, capacity, intention'.[66]

The link between fear and exorcistic manoeuvre is laid
bare in Malte's meditation on 'Der Einsame'. In this
generalized form, he sums up his fear of engulfment by
others, interpreting the intercourse which 'consumes' him as
hostility: 'Sie haben nie einen Einsamen gesehen, sie haben
ihn nur gehaßt, ohne ihn zu kennen. Sie sind seine Nachbaren
gewesen, die ihn aufbrauchten' (VI,879). The theme of
hostility is then developed at length, with echoes of the
'suffering servant', but the passage concludes:

> Aber dann, wenn er nicht aufsah, besannen sie sich.
> Sie ahnten, daß sie mit alledem seinen Willen
> taten; daß sie ihn in seinem Alleinsein bestärkten
> und ihm halfen, sich abzuschneiden von ihnen für
> immer. Und nun schlugen sie um und wandten das
> Letzte an, das Äußerste, den anderen Widerstand:
> den Ruhm. Und bei diesem Lärmen blickte fast jeder
> auf und wurde zerstreut. (VI,880)

The meditation suggests more than the *topos* of the misunderstood artist. The pattern of a reversal of values, an acceptance of 'Alleinsein' as an identity in itself, mirrors the repeated assertion that acceptance of fear would, if Malte were only capable of it, become a paradoxical transformation of fear - a theme which has deeper roots than strategies of 'silence, exile and cunning'. In the ensuing memories of stories read in childhood, moreover, it is developed in a more general manner, not specifically related to the artist. Malte remembers few of the details of the story of Grischa Otrepjow, the false Czar, but what seems to him significant is not the event which precipitated his downfall - his betrayal - but rather the *recognition* which should have ensured his survival. Malte wonders 'ob aber seine Unsicherheit nicht gerade damit begann, daß sie ihn anerkannte?' His conclusion, that 'die Kraft seiner Verwandlung hätte darin beruht, niemandes Sohn mehr zu sein', is generalized in a marginal note which prefigures the dénouement of the novel: '(Das ist schließlich die Kraft aller jungen Leute, die fortgegangen sind)' (VI,882). Malte's analysis of the sources of Grischa's strength forms a close parallel with Laing's analysis of the cultivation of false and inner self. Grischa's adoption of the false self of the Czar enables him, behind this mask, to be 'freier und unbegrenzter in seinen Möglichkeiten', whilst recognition of this false self as true by a third party - even as conscious deceit - diminishes this boundless possibility, which he recovers only in the moment between downfall and death:

> Ob es gesagt wird oder nicht, man muß darauf schwören, daß zwischen Stimme und Pistolenschuß, unendlich zusammengedrängt, noch einmal Wille und Macht in ihm war, alles zu sein. (VI,884)

The 'inner' self is apprehended as 'endless possibility,

capacity, intention', so long as it is hidden behind a false
self which protects the 'elusive, transcendent' inner core
from recognition and engulfment.

It is not of course Rilke's private biography which is
in question here, nor even inner strategies played out by
his fictional protagonist. These manoeuvres exist at a
purely hypothetical level in the series of alternative
selves which Malte, himself Rilke's 'anti-self', projects
against the backcloth of his anxieties in the second part of
the novel. The diagnosis and aspiration expressed in the
present tense in the meditation on 'Der Einsame' is transposed into a historical dimension before it is concretized
in the figure of Otrepjow - a manoeuvre which both
emphasizes the unavailability of Otrepjow's experience for
Malte himself, and represents Malte's plight as characteristic of modern life. Near the opening of the novel, the
critique of mass-production death in Paris hospitals leads
back to the death of the old Chamberlain as representing a
mode of existence which, Malte feels, has not passed
completely beyond availability. But the counterpoints
become more and more remote as the work proceeds. Malte's
childhood experience of anxiety in the dressing-up scene is
answered across the pages of the book, across years of
Malte's life, and across centuries of history, by the firm-
ness of identity of the otherwise pathetic figure of Charles
VI, condemned to spend his life playing cards, but finding
security in the knowledge 'daß auch er eine bestimmte Karte
sei, vielleicht eine schlechte, eine zornig ausgespielte, die
immer verlor: aber immer die gleiche: aber nie eine andere'
(VI,911).

The most significant of these transpositions concerns
the figure of Abelone, already an inhabitant of Malte's
distant childhood rather than of his 'present' world.

Abelone appears first as a figure mystifying to the child,
because she stands outside the expected pattern of relationships - a link with 'Der Einsame' and Grischa Otrepjow. But
this first mention is merely occasion for the narrative to
move into the more distant realms of the Boussac tapestries,
whilst her second appearance in Malte's musings serves to
introduce a discussion of Bettine von Arnim's letters, and
it is this more remote figure which replaces the known person
as catalyst of Malte's meditations and guide, Beatrice-like,
towards the conclusion. 'Nein, Bettine ist wirklicher,
Abelone, die ich gekannt habe, war wie eine Vorbereitung auf
sie'(VI,897). The transposition from known to historical
figure is accompanied by a transposition of the whole tone
of the work from the world of Malte's Paris to the mythical
world of 'Orpheus. Eurydike. Hermes'. For Eurydice's
'Hingegebenheit', her immersion in the natural order, is
Bettine's too, and Malte thinks of this quality as one which
confers 'death' even on the life of Bettine:

> Sie hat von Anfang an sich im Ganzen so ausgebreitet,
> als wär sie nach ihrem Tod. Überall hat sie sich ganz
> weit ins Sein hineingelegt, zugehörig dazu, und was ihr
> geschah, das war ewig in der Natur; dort erkannte sie
> sich und löste sich beinah schmerzhaft heraus... (VI,897)

Indeed, Bettine's 'mythical' qualities exceed even those of
Eurydice; it is rather the roses of 'Die Rosenschale' which
provide the model for the outward-going, transforming power
of her love:

> Oder ist nicht die Welt überhaupt von dir? denn wie oft
> hast du sie in Brand gesteckt mit deiner Liebe und hast
> sie lodern sehen und aufbrennen und hast sie heimlich
> durch eine andere ersetzt, wenn alle schliefen.

And, as in the case of the roses, this quality is allied to
its apparent opposite, a fulfilled self-containment

paradoxically derived from the unfulfilment of her love:

> Was heißt es, daß er nicht hat erwidern können?
> Solche Liebe bedarf keiner Erwiderung, sie hat
> Lockruf und Antwort in sich; sie erhört sich selbst.
>
> (VI,898)

From this point on, praise of the unrequited lover becomes the major recurrent motif of the novel, as the narrative
moves sinuously through figures from Froissart - 'Reminizsensen
seiner Belesenheit' which weave further arabesques on questions
of identity - through meditations on the theatres at Orange and
the actress Eleonora Duse - permitting further interplay of masks
and selves - to 'die Portugiesin', to Héloïse, to Gaspara
Stampa, and finally to the most remote figure of all -
Byblos, who followed Kaunos to the end of her strength:

> aber so stark war ihres Wesens Bewegtheit, daß sie,
> hinsinkend, jenseits vom Tod als Quelle wiedererschien,
> eilend, als eilende Quelle. (VI,925)

At the same time, the ironic counterpart is generalized in
a language which approaches once again that of *Das Buch von
der Armut und vom Tode*. Where Byblos achieved fullness and
absorption into the natural order, 'wir', the modern Every-
man, are excluded from the cycle of the seasons, from
blooming and giving fruit. 'Wir können nicht fertig werden.
Wir rücken unsere Natur hinaus' (VI,926).

Departing once more via 'Mädchen in meiner Heimat' and
Louise Labé, the narrative reaches back to Sappho, returns
to the present day with a Danish girl's song of unrequited
love, and finally comes to rest with Abelone and a further
restatement of the central theme, this time in a quasi-
theological mode:

Manchmal früher fragte ich mich, warum Abelone die
Kalorien ihres großartigen Gefühls nicht an Gott
wandte. Ich weiß, sie sehnte sich, ihrer Liebe alles
Transitive zu nehmen, aber könnte ihr wahrhaftiges
Herz sich darüber täuschen, daß Gott nur eine Richtung
der Liebe ist, kein Liebesgegenstand? Wußte sie
nicht, daß keine Gegenliebe von ihm zu fürchten war?
                                            (VI,937)

Such a mode of discourse reaches back even beyond *Das Buch
von der Armut und vom Tode* to *Das Buch vom mönchischen Leben*;
but Malte's marginal note, in its terse finality, points unmistakably to the existential roots of Rilke's rather
preciously nuanced 'theology':

> (Geliebtsein heißt aufbrennen. Lieben ist: Leuchten
> mit unerschöpflichem Öle. Geliebtwerden ist vergehen,
> Lieben ist dauern.) (VI,937)

The one half of the axiom corresponds to Malte's fears of
'engulfment' in intercourse with others; the other half his
fears of loss of identity. The tenaciously pursued figure
of the unrequited lover, like the 'theology' of *Das Stundenbuch*, offers a paradoxically positive evaluation of
intrinsically defensive strategies.

But the distance between this idealized form and the
actual experience of Malte is too great for the celebration
of the unrequited lover to escape an ironic overtone. It is
the task of the concluding section of the book, the re-
telling of the parable of the Prodigal, to rework the
aspirations expressed in the figure of the unrequited lover
into a form which might answer his own situation less indirectly. For the Prodigal, in Malte's version, is an
amalgam of the felt experience of 'Der Einsame', as a
generalized formulation of Malte's own experience, and the
ideal, but impossibly remote, experience of Byblos, Louise
Labé or Gaspara Stampa. Just as Malte sees recognition as

disastrous for 'Der Einsame', so the Prodigal distrusts
'Teilnahme, Erwartung und Besorgtheit' even on the part of
the dogs (VI,938). And his decision to leave home recalls
the marginal note to the story of Grischa Otrepjow. On the
other hand, the Prodigal strives consciously towards that
condition of 'Lieben' without 'Geliebtsein' described as
the triumph of the unrequited lover. He learns slowly 'den
geliebten Gegenstand mit den Strahlen seines Gefühls zu
durchscheinen, statt ihn darin zu verzehren' (VI,941), and
eventually to offer his love to God, 'die stille, ziellose
Arbeit' (VI,943). This time, Malte tells us, he hoped for
requital. Since a few pages earlier he had insisted that no
requital is to be feared from God, the sense can only be
that he aspired towards that reversal where 'Lockruf'
becomes 'Antwort', portrayed in the figures of Bettine and
Sappho. The results of his striving are ambiguous. At a
certain point he feels it necessary to return home to 'take
on again' his childhood, and we do not know, Malte comments,
whether he stayed or departed again. What we are left with
is a gesture, the gesture with which he greeted his family,

> seine Gebärde, die unerhörte Gebärde, die man nie
> vorher gesehen hatte; die Gebärde des Flehens, mit
> der er sich an ihre Füsse warf, sie beschwörend,
> daß sie nicht liebten. (VI,945)

The emphasis falls heavily on one side of the equation, on
'Nicht-Geliebtsein' rather than 'Lieben'. As for the
latter, we know that the Prodigal had turned his love to
God, and the work concludes:

> Er war jetzt furchtbar schwer zu lieben, und er
> fühlte, daß nur Einer dazu imstande sei. Der aber
> wollte noch nicht. (VI,946)

The reversal in which love would turn into a 'Geliebtsein'

65

which would not consume, 'Lockruf' into 'Antwort', has not
happened.

Earlier, in his childhood, Malte had experienced what
he calls 'die innige Indifferenz seines Herzens',

> die ihn manchmal früh in den Feldern mit solcher
> Reinheit ergriff, daß er zu laufen begann, um nicht
> Zeit und Atem zu haben, mehr zu sein als ein leichter
> Moment, in dem der Morgen zum Bewußtsein kommt. (VI,938-9)

This elusive, transcendent self is something which the
Prodigal comes slowly to recover in his years of exile, when
he feels 'allgemein und anonym...wie ein zögernd Genesender'
(VI,942). This inner self of 'endless possibility, capacity,
intention' requires, as an existential imperative, to be
protected from engulfment: the Prodigal's gesture represents
that imperative. To be *celebrated*, positively evaluated, it
requires a direction which, however, must not appear in a
visible form, for the world of action and intercourse belong
to the false selves. 'Leuchten mit unerschöpflichem Öle' -
from Eurydice through rose-bowl to Prodigal Rilke seeks
formulations of a condition which allies an outward-streaming
energy to its opposite, a closed self-containment. In many
of his formulations, the paradox is resolved on a transcendental plane, and allied with an aspiration towards an
intuitive harmony with the natural order; the inner self,
cut off by its nature from relationships with the world of
experience and with other subjectivities, claims direct
access to 'das Leben', 'die Erde', God or Nature. In others,
it is endowed with a creative, transforming power which,
though devoid of 'content', affirms its ontological
substantiality. The nuancing and paradoxes of Rilke's early
verse, the 'Totsein' of Eurydice, the indirections of the
Neue Gedichte, the paradoxical celebration of the unrequited

lover - all these represent so many manoeuvres to permit
celebration to arise out of deep-rooted anxiety.

If the conclusion of *Malte Laurids Brigge* differs
substantially from earlier formulations, it is principally
in the fact that, perhaps partly by reason of his adoption
of the novel form, Rilke lays bare in much more explicit
form - indeed with, up to a certain point, an extraordinary
degree of insight - the anxieties which underlay his work
from the beginning, and renounces the easy route of taking
aspiration for achievement, allowing the work to close in
uncertainty, with a negative and anxious note incarnated in
the gesture of the Prodigal. To close the circle from 'Vor
lauter Lauschen' to 'Atmen, du unsichtbares Gedicht', whilst
not by-passing the insights of *Malte Laurids Brigge*, was the
task lying before him.

IV. STRATEGIES OF DISPLACEMENT

Album de vers anciens,
Introduction à la méthode de Léonard de Vinci,
La Soirée avec M. Teste.

Valéry's early verse is on the whole justly neglected.
The stock-in-trade of late Parnassian and Symbolist poetry
is more conspicuous than any identifiable personal voice,
while the course of development of Valéry's early experience
is obscured by the later reworking of many early poems for
the *Album de vers anciens*. Certain configurations lurking
beneath the fin-de-siècle surface are however of interest,
and a tendency to blur the traces is, as will be seen, an
important factor in the interpretation of these configurations.

The choice between Parnassian and Symbolist models
signified, among other things, a choice between first-person
and third-person lyrical forms. Valéry's earliest recover-
able lyric is in this sense entirely in the Symbolist mould,
and demonstrates a characteristically Symbolist literary
sensibility:

> Et moi, mélancolique amant de l'onde sombre...
> (I,1573)
> L'ombre venait, les fleurs s'ouvraient, rêvait mon
> Âme... (I,1574)
> Car, j'aime cette grève où mon ombre s'allonge...
> (I,1576)

It is noticeable that, among those poems which can be dated
with some certainty to the 1890s, and which survive into the
Album, only one preserves this alliance of first-person discourse and elegiac melancholy, in which the world around the
speaker is absorbed into his own mood:

> A travers les bois bleus et les bras fraternels,
> Une tendre lueur d'heure ambiguë existe,
> Et d'un reste du jour me forme un fiancé
> Nu, sur la place pâle où m'attire l'eau triste...
>
> (I,82)

That poem is, moreover, placed in the mouth of a familiar
legendary character, Narcissus, giving, as it were, an
'objective' justification to the tonality. The other poem
which utilizes a similar first person technique, 'Hélène',
joined later by 'Air de Sémiramis', is radically different
in tone.[67] Helen's

> Azur! c'est moi... Je viens des grottes de la mort
> Entendre l'onde se rompre aux degrés sonores...
>
> (I,76)

initiates an energetic upward movement echoed by Sémiramis's

> - Je réponds!... Je surgis de ma profonde absence!
>
> (I,92)

The *characteristic* form of the *Album* is pictorial or dramatic,
with a third-person protagonist set in a described scene, the
poet himself remaining in the background. And the characteristic configuration of these poems is different from either
the elegiac absorption of world into mood found in 'Narcisse
parle' and earlier verse, or the masterful separateness of
Helen or Semiramis.

The Pre-Raphaelite spinner of 'La Fileuse' dreams,
intoxicated by the hum of the wheel, but the poet's eyes are
open. The broad outlines of the poem may betray the young

poet's admiration for Mallarmé, the 'croisée' and other
quasi-symbolic elements recalling 'Les Fenêtres' and the
'salut vain' of the rose both 'Prose' and 'Toast Funèbre'.
But, Symbolist though the work may be in its tenuous but
thoroughly Mallarméan association of purity and extinction,
its surface remains linked to sensation and impression. It
is not simply that the 'tige, où le vent vagabond se repose'
is more concrete than the stylized 'cent iris' of 'Prose';
it is also that the opening of the poem renders both more
directly and more succinctly the hypnotic effect of the light
and heat of 'l'azur' than Mallarmé's more purely symbolic poem
of that name. Even through the precious vocabulary, one
senses Valéry's fascination with 'la matière des choses: eau,
roche, pulpe des feuilles, le sable très fin, la chair'
(II,1507):

> Lasse, ayant bu l'azur, de filer l'agneline
>   Chevelure, à ses doigts si faibles évasive...
>   (I,1534)

The reverie of Narcissus is *displaced* into the second-person
protagonist, whom the poet watches, framed 'au bleu de la
croisée', 'de lumière ceinte'.

Images of unreality may themselves be more or less
'real'. The subject of 'La Belle au bois dormant' (first
version of 'Au Bois dormant') invites a dream of unreal
purity, but that unreality is capable of absorbing evocative
detail - the birds pecking at the rings, drops of dew fall-
ing into flowers - which are 'observed' by the poet, not the
princess in her 'nonchalante idylle' (I,1546). In his brief
but valuable account of the *Vers anciens*, Marcel Raymond
notes:

> Ce qui importe, c'est d'essayer de ressusciter dans le
> langage l'impression, avec sa fraîcheur et sa teneur
> *ontologique*.[68]

Frequently, and increasingly, what distinguishes Valéry's
juvenilia from that of other would-be Mallarméans is not a
closer adherence to the 'tentation platonicienne' of the
Master, but rather an attempt to seek 'un contact profond et
réel avec les choses'.[69] In the 'Naissance de Vénus', this
search takes the form of a conception of the goddess's birth
as an emergence from 'la matière des choses':

> Les graviers d'or qu'arrose sa marche gracile
> Croulent sous ses pieds fins et la grève facile
> Garde les frais baisers de ses pas puérils.
>
> Et le golfe a laissé dans ses yeux fous et vagues
> Où dort le souvenir des mobiles périls
> L'eau riante, et la danse infidèle des vagues!
>
> (I,1541)

'Baignée', surviving almost unchanged from its 1892 version
into the *Album*, is marked by a close attention to sensuous
detail with no detour through mythological subject-matter or
ostensible concern with more distant ideals. Again, it is
through the protagonist that the poet communicates a sense
of delicious abandon in contact with the physical reality of
water and air:

> Un bras vague, inondé dans le néant limpide
> Pour une ombre de fleur à cueillir doucement
> S'effile, ondule, oublie en le délice vide,
>
> Si l'autre courbé pur sous le beau firmament
> Parmi la chevelure immense qu'il humecte
> Capture dans l'or simple un vol ivre d'insecte.
>
> (I,1545)

The *poet's* presence is marked by a detached and painterly
eye:

> Isolant la torsade où je figure un casque
> La tête d'or scintille...

Two poems of a few years later accentuate rather than

71

radically alter this already characteristic configuration.
In 'Été', the girl lying on the sand is 'invaded' by the
physical realities surrounding her:

> ...ardente ruche
> De mer éparpillée en mille mouches sur
> Les touffes d'une chair fraîche comme une cruche
> Et jusque dans la bouche où se mouille l'azur...
>
> (I,1564)

Her very sleep is 'poreux'; both body and consciousness are
'open' to the world about:

> ...les épaules, le sein mûr
> Sous les meules de brise aux écumeuses roues
> Brûlent abandonnés autour du vase obscur
> Où filtrent les grands bruits...

In 'Anne', the assault of male desire is replaced, as she
falls asleep, by the even more intimate violence of the air
and neighbouring sea:

> Et comme un souvenir pressant ses propres chairs,
> Une bouche brisée et pleine d'eau brûlante
> Roule le goût immense et le reflet des mers.(I,89)

In both poems, the interpenetration of protagonist and scene
is echoed by a vision of the exterior scene itself as interpenetration and transformation of its different elements:

> Et toi, maison brûlante, espace, cher espace
> Tranquille, où l'arbre fume et perd quelques
> oiseaux,
> Où crève infiniment la rumeur de la masse
> De la mer...   (I,1565)
> Et sur le linge où l'aube insensible se plisse...
> Mais suave, de l'arbre extérieur, la palme
> Vaporeuse remue au delà du remords,
> Et dans le feu, parmi trois feuilles, l'oiseau
> calme
> Commence le chant...   (I,90,91)

Raymond, commenting on the 'alchimie verbale' of the
Vers anciens, maintains that it is sustained by 'une
conscience aiguë des mouvements du corps dans le monde, du
corps poreux et pénétrable, assimilable au monde'.[70] It
should be added that the assimilation of body to world is
two-fold: the protagonist's bodies - and consciousnesses -
are seen as subject to an intimate interpenetration with the
physical world about them, indeed. But that interpenetration, displaced from the lyrical interpenetration of
world and self in 'Narcisse parle', is assimilated by the
detached poetic eye to a system of interpenetration *in* the
world. Body and sensibility become part of a world of metamorphosis, which is however not inhabited by the poetic 'je',
whose stance before it is radically separate to the point of
a form of intellectual *voyeurisme*.

> Un feu distinct m'habite, et je vois froidement
> La violente vie illuminée entière...   (I,81)

The lines are difficult to date, but even if retrospective,
they constitute an illuminating summary of the tensions of
Valéry's earliest work.

    *   *   *   *   *   *   *   *

It is part of a certain myth about Valéry that the
crisis of 1892 provoked a total rupture in his literary
career, and that the works associated with that crisis, the
Introduction à la méthode de Léonard de Vinci of 1895 and
La Soirée avec M. Teste of 1896, fix an unbridgeable gulf
between all earlier work and that which followed after a
period of silence. The truth of the matter is more complex.
An accentuation of already existing configurations has been
observed between the earlier poems of the *Album* and those
written towards the close of the decade, and that accentuation may be associated closely with the two prose-works

which, in different ways, spell out the tensions underlying
the verse.

> L'homme universel [Valéry notes in the *Introduction*]
> commence, lui aussi, par contempler simplement, et il
> revient toujours à s'imprégner de spectacles. Il
> retourne aux ivresses de l'instinct particulier et à
> l'émotion que donne la moindre chose réelle. (I,1164f.)

One aspect of the development of this theme is defined in a
marginal note of 1930 as 'conservation de la subtilité et de
l'instabilité sensorielles':

> La plupart des gens y voient par l'intellect bien plus
> souvent que par les yeux. Au lieu d'espaces colorés,
> ils prennent connaissance de concepts... Sachant
> horizontal le niveau des eaux tranquilles, ils
> méconnaissent que la mer est *debout* au fond de la
> vue... (I,1165,6)

There could be no better commentary on 'Été, roche d'air
pur...', on the young poet's attempt to bypass conventional
visual response in favour of the directness of sense-
impression. If, however, 'Été' and other poems make a
sharp, though implicit, distinction between the response of
the *sensibility* to sense-impression - displaced into a
second or third-person protagonist - and the response of
the *intellect* or the purely visual *imagination* - detached
and observant - the *Introduction* makes the distinction
explicit and complete. The response of sensibility is
dismissed in the picture of 'Nature' as 'éruption verte,
vague et continue' (I,1167), while the response celebrated
is that of the 'vertige de l'analogie' (I,1169), the power
of imaginative transformation working on the purely visual
details of the surrounding world:

> Puis, à son gré, il arrange et défait ses impressions
> successives. Il peut apprécier d'étranges

combinaisons: il regarde comme un être total et solide
un groupe de fleurs ou d'hommes, une main, une joue
qu'il isole, une tache de clarté sur un mur, une
rencontre d'animaux mêlés par hasard. (I,1168f.)

'Telle...', he concludes, 'expire l'ivresse de ces
choses particulières, desquelles il n'y a pas de science'
(I,1170). The world is apprehended as a series of *discontinuous* figures, broken off from the 'éruption...
continue' of 'Nature', and whose re-integration into
continuity is a function of *analysis*:

   ...l'esprit n'a fait qu'agrandir ses fonctions, créer
   des êtres selon les problèmes que toute sensation lui
   pose et qu'il résout plus ou moins aisément... (I,1171)

In this perspective, the 'ivresse de l'instinct particulier';
'l'émotion que donne la moindre chose réelle' are reduced to
an abstract conception, 'la facilité ou la difficulté
qu'elles offrent à notre compréhension' (I,1171).

In the exuberant pages of the *Introduction*, this epiphenomenal power of analysis and transformation exists in a
dialectical relationship with 'ces formes toutes quel-
conques' - among which, Valéry adds, 'son propre corps se
compte' (I,1168). Moreover, little though Valéry's hypothetical hero may have to do with the historical Leonardo,
the dialectic itself leads back into the world through the
constructions to which it gives birth. In *La Soirée avec
M. Teste*, both movements are short-circuited. Before even
meeting the hero, the narrator is taken with the idea that
the production of works of art, or indeed of any 'works',
is not only of lesser value than the mind which produces
them, but even detracts from the power of that mind:

   Pour s'étonner de lui, il faut le voir, - et pour être
   vu il faut qu'il se montre. Et il me montre que la

75

> niaise manie de son nom le possède. Ainsi, chaque
> grand homme est taché d'une erreur; (II,15f.)

Teste is one who has refused such impurity:

> Si cet homme avait changé l'objet de ses méditations
> fermées, s'il eût tourné contre le monde la puissance
> régulière de son esprit, rien ne lui eût résisté.
>
> (II,19)

The characterization is in itself similar to Malte's
analysis of 'Der Einsame', but again, though in a different
way, the motif is more than a hyperbolic celebration of the
solitude of the creative mind. For Teste's meditations are
'fermées' in a more fundamental sense. Of 'l'homme
universel', the *Introduction* says that 'il est fait pour
n'oublier rien de ce qui entre dans la confusion de ce qui
est; nul arbuste' (I,1155). Of Teste, the narrator reports
that 'il ne perdait pas un atome de tout ce qui devenait
sensible' (II,21). But this universal attentiveness is
ultimately *reflexive*.

Teste has suppressed the inner drama; 'il avait *tué la
marionnette*', as the narrator puts it:

> Qu'avait-il fait de sa personnalité? Comment se
> voyait-il?...Jamais il ne riait, jamais un air de
> malheur sur son visage. Il haïssait la mélancolie.
>
> (II,18)

In the *Vers anciens*, we have seen 'melancholy' displaced and
then abolished, and the inner drama displaced into second or
third-person protagonists. In the *Introduction*, the inner
drama is largely ignored, and relegated to an object of
analysis, subject to the same laws of continuity and period-
icity as the outer world. In the evening at the theatre
which forms the centre-piece of the *Soirée*, it is displaced,
first on to the stage, and secondly on to the reactions of
the audience, which Teste observes without sharing:

76

M. Teste dit: 'Le suprême *les* simplifie. Je parie
qu'ils pensent tous, de plus en plus, *vers* la même
chose. Ils seront égaux devant la crise ou limite
commune. Du reste, la loi n'est pas si simple...
puisqu'elle me néglige, - et - je suis ici.' (II,21)

The narrator himself, like the protagonist of the early
verse, is relegated to the status of object of analysis,
'confondu avec les choses...reculé, mêlé aux maisons, aux
grandeurs de l'espace, au coloris remué de la rue, aux
coins...' (II,18). In the conversation on the way home
from the theatre, he takes the part of sensibility:

Pourtant, *répondis-je*, comment se soustraire à une
musique si puissante! Et pourquoi? J'y trouve une
ivresse particulière, dois-je la dédaigner?...Nierez-
vous qu'il y ait des choses anasthésiques? Des arbres
qui saoulent, des hommes qui donnent de la force, des
filles qui paralysent, des ciels qui coupent la
parole?' (II,22)

But Teste will have none of this:

'Eh! Monsieur! que m'importe le 'talent' de vos arbres
- et des autres!... Je suis chez MOI, je parle ma
langue, je hais les choses extraordinaires.

He not only hates extraordinary things; he also contrives to
sterilize their extraordinariness. In the *Introduction*
Valéry had reduced 'things' to 'la facilité ou la difficulté
qu'elles offrent à notre compréhension'; Teste repeats this
reduction, adding the impatient comment: 'Et que m'importe
ce que je sais fort bien?' (II,19). Ultimately, he is
interested in one thing only, and falls asleep on the
thought: 'Je suis étant, et me voyant; me voyant me voir, et
ainsi de suite...' (II,25). The sentence forms the final
link in a chain of displacements which push the 'inner
drama' of sensibility at ever further removes from the
centre of the self.

In the face of the 'quelconque' of Teste's room, with

its 'morne mobilier abstrait' (II,23), the narrator
shudders: 'J'eus peur de l'infinie tristesse possible dans
ce lieu pur et banal'. Though he eschews the public face
of literary or other works, Teste *has* a public face, behind
which lurks that 'infinie tristesse' which the narrator
suspects, and into which the reader is given a glimpse in
the closing pages. His indifference for his surroundings,
or rather his hatred of the extraordinary, and thus his
preference for the 'quelconque', prepares the way for a
particular kind of 'ennui', a nostalgia for a reality un-
touched by the deadening attentiveness of his own mind:

> Maintenant, je me sais par coeur. Le coeur aussi.
> Bah! toute la terre est marquée, tous les pavillons
> couvrent tous les territoires... Reste mon lit.
> J'aime ce courant de sommeil et de linge: ce linge
> qui se tend et se plisse, ou se froisse... (II,24)

Moreover, Teste suffers, and in pain sensibility finds its
Trojan horse. The body, displaced from the self to become
part of that external world which Teste reduces to the
mirror of his own consciousness, enters once more into an
intimate and mysterious alliance with consciousness:

> Quand *cela* va venir, je trouve en moi quelque chose
> de confus ou de diffus. Il se fait dans mon être
> des endroits... brumeux...Je combats tout, - hors la
> souffrance de mon corps, au delà d'une certaine
> grandeur. (II,25)

The narrator also suspects 'des sentiments qui me
faisaient frémir, une terrible *obstination* dans des
expériences enivrantes' (II,18; my italics). Among the
musings on which Teste falls asleep is the fragment:
'Les bras d'une Berthe, s'ils prennent de l'importance, je
suis volé, - comme par la douleur...' (II,25). Teste's
obstinacy, his hatred of the extraordinary, his fear of

sensibility as violation, all suggest a certain internal
'Caligulism' in his mental discipline. And it is difficult
not to see the series of displacements through which
Valéry's early work proceeds as ultimately defensive in
motivation, designed to create an ever more rigorous
separation of an 'ungraspable, elusive, transcendent' inner
self from a 'false self' embodied in the world. Hartmut
Köhler has accumulated numerous passages from Valéry's early
Cahiers bearing witness to a 'despotisme personnel' directed
against 'Moi trop sensible', as, for example, the following
entry:

> Je ne m'abandonne jamais. Je ne le puis. Trace
> définitive, peut-être, d'un souci maternel, toujours
> présent jadis et ressenti par moi. Tous les sentiments
> modifiés en moi par ce non-abandon. Pas d'ivresse que
> brève et vite inquiétée. Sur toute chose je crains de
> m'engager. Il arrive alors que si quelque impression
> trop forte me veut à tout prix, il faut qu'elle soit
> vaincue et je la fuis physiquement par évanouissement.
> Je nous détruis ensemble.[71]

Our concern here is not however with the personal roots
of Valéry's early texts. To dwell overlong on them would
obscure the equally important fact that, whatever the
existential basis for the *Soirée*, its transposition into a
certain form of discourse was to have far-reacing
consequences. For the moment, it is the configurations of
Valéry's work as they stand at this stage which concerns us,
both in contrast with those disclosed in Rilke's work, and
as background to the later configurations glimpsed in 'Les
Pas'.

As for the first, there are a number of curious
similarities between Teste and Malte. Most marked at first
sight is a certain unorthodox but profound radicalism. Both
refuse, and hold in horror, the *facile*. Malte, repudiating

his earlier work, sets himself a task neglected by centuries of humanity; Teste asks insistently 'Que peut un homme', and dismisses all previous efforts of apparent genius. From the 'quelconque' of their respective Paris apartments, both set out on an adventure the cost of which is incalculable to their own selves, and both are apparently denied the full fruits of their efforts.

But the essential is not there. Rilke took two years to understand *La Soirée*; having penetrated its secrets, however, he then added it to his personal canon of Valéry's works. This reaction is indicative of the play of contrasts and similarities which must both be given due weight in any comparison with *Die Aufzeichnungen*. In one sense, Malte takes up where Teste leaves off: Teste's defeat is in pain and the demands of sensibility; Malte commences his quest by opening himself fully to the pain within and without and to the overwhelming demands of his own empathy. But the two works taken together form a circle; crushed by the magnitude of his task, Malte reverts to the position from which Teste starts, the Prodigal's refusal of love echoing Teste's refusal of 'les bras d'une Berthe'. Teste is convinced of his own superiority: the narrator of *La Soirée*, avowedly 'inferior' to its hero, commences with the words, 'La bêtise n'est pas mon fort'. Malte feels crushed in advance by his own nothingness. Yet out of these differing estimations of themselves, Teste out of an (apparent, but perhaps assumed) self-confidence, Malte out of desperate anxiety, the two protagonists illustrate a common aspiration, for Teste the only and highest good, for Malte a *pis aller* - a closed self-sufficiency. Their common gesture is one of refusal, dismissive in one case, anxious in the other, but in either case defensive, fending off all encroachments on the core of the self.

It can hardly be doubted that the form of discourse represented by a work like *La Soirée* - the sketch, as Valéry later defined it, of 'un Hippogriffe, une Chimère de la mythologie intellectuelle', in a language 'forcé, parfois énergiquement abstrait' (II,14) - must have represented for Rilke a powerful barrier, obscuring the partly veiled, partly transcended, existential drama behind the work (as indeed, it has obscured it for many over-hasty critics, ignoring the presence of the narrator, and identifying Teste as simply an idealized portrait of Valéry, the arch-intellectual). But the displacement of existential into quasi-philosophical is an important aspect of the work, as is in general Valéry's ability, which Rilke did not share, to analyse intellectually his own mechanisms of defence. In one sense, the displacements of Valéry's early works are both defensive, and contain the possibilities of a transcendence of defensiveness.

In his analyses of the *Cahiers*, Köhler has also defined the obverse of the Testean version of the self as 'elusive, transcendent' - the self as 'endless possibility, capacity, intention', as *Protée*, in Valéry's own words:

> Le conflit de souvenir, du *nom*, des habitudes, des penchants, de la forme mirée, de l'être arrêté, fixé, inscrit de l'histoire, du *particulier* avec - le centre universel, la capacité de changement, la jeunesse éternelle de l'oubli, le Protée, l'être qui ne peut être enchaîné, le mouvement tournant, la fonction renaissante, le moi qui peut être entièrement nouveau et même multiple...[72]

In Rilke, this 'endless possibility' is characterized as a creative, transforming power, devoid of 'content', but affirmed ontologically by being constantly linked to a transcendental plane on which the circle is closed once more between self-sufficiency and outward-streaming energy. In Valéry's early prose-works, there is a certain tendency to

view the inner, 'pure' consciousness as epiphenomenal,
'transcendental' in Husserl's sense, but from the outset
Valéry refuses transcendence in Rilke's pantheistic sense.
If Proteus represents a power of transformation, it is
transformation of the *self*. Hints of this possibility
appear in *La Soirée*: Teste is 'l'être absorbé dans sa
variation' (II,18), but only within the limits of his own
closed, short-circuited circle, the 'variation' being thrown
into insignificance by contrast with the emphasis on the
fixed, central point. Of the configuration of 'Les Pas',
Valéry's early work offers the *elements* - the inner drama
of sensibility, its 'porosity' to the external world, and
the detachment of the observing self. But the 'porosity'
is refused, the inner drama displaced and disconnected from
the core of the self, which is treated as autonomous and
self-sufficient. These elements would require a radical
re-assembly before they could offer Rilke an example for the
re-configuration of his own work.

V. THE CRITICAL YEARS

Rilke's work from 1912 to 1922

The most immediately striking characteristic of the
opening lines of the *Duineser Elegien* is their syntactical
form. Four subjunctive verbs frame two hypotheses, the
first cast as rhetorical question, the implied answer to
which undermines the very basis of the second:

> Wer, wenn ich schriee, hörte mich denn aus der
> Engel
> Ordungen? und gesetzt selbst, es nähme
> einer mich plötzlich ans Herz: ich verginge von
> seinem
> stärkeren Dasein. (EI,1)

Thus one essential feature of the cycle was proclaimed at
its inception in 1912 - its exploratory nature, its awareness of ironic undercutting of its own speculations. And
in this dizzying perspective are set two protagonists - an
'ich' whose sole known content is an impulse to cry out,
and an ordered impassivity designated as 'angelic'. In the
second Elegy, the one interrogates the other - 'Wer seid
ihr?' - and supplies its own answers:

> Frühe Geglückte, ihr Verwöhnten der Schöpfung,
> Höhenzüge, morgenrötliche Grate
> aller Erschaffung, - Pollen der blühenden Gott-
> heit,
> Gelenke des Lichtes, Gänge, Treppen, Throne,
> Räume aus Wesen, Schilde aus Wonne, Tumulte
> stürmisch entzückten Gefühls und plötzlich, ein-
> zeln,

> *Spiegel*: die die entströmte eigene Schönheit
> wiederschöpfen zurück in das eigene Antlitz.
> (EII,10)

The very *form* of the description - cumulative, and
marked by an evocative combination of the abstract and the
concrete - is reminiscent of 'Die Rosenschale':

> Lautloses Leben, Aufgehn ohne Ende,
> Raum-brauchen ohne Raum von jenem Raum
> zu nehmen, den die Dinge rings verringern,
> fast nicht Umrissen-sein wie Ausgespartes
> und lauter Inneres, viel seltsam Zartes
> und Sich-bescheinendes... (I,552)

The paradoxical combination of perfect self-containment
with outward-streaming radiance seen in the roses is here
raised to a mythical level. Mythical, because it is soon
apparent that the angelic condition is defined by its
contrast with the human. The 'stärkeres Dasein' of the
angels is a symbolic manner of commenting on human lack of
'being'; their absorption into the natural order, as
'Verwöhnte der Schöpfung', a mode of awareness of the
alienation of the human from the natural. The qualities
of roses could, by a detour, be 'ours', but those same
qualities in the angels are by definition not available.
Thus a second major characteristic of the Elegies is
announced; by the fact of having incarnated in these
mythical figures, defined as what we are not, the precise
qualities which his earlier work had seen as above all
desirable, Rilke makes inevitable a more radical critique
of human consciousness than ever before.

From these bleak premises, the first two Elegies of
1912 move in two directions. The first commences with
those 'fragments shored against our ruins', the sensation
evoked by natural objects which suggests that the natural

order from which we are divorced is yet not entirely
foreign to us:

> ...Es bleibt uns vielleicht
> irgend ein Baum an dem Abhang...
> O und die Nacht, die Nacht, wenn der Wind voller
> uns am Angesicht zehrt... Weltraum
> Ja, die Frühlinge brauchten dich wohl. Es muteten
> Sterne dir zu... (EI,13) manche

We are distracted from the 'Auftrag' presented by this
intuition - distracted by the limiting perspective, the
lack of disinterestedness, of the human condition. And so
the Elegy turns towards those figures - the unrequited lover,
the young dead - which offer possibilities of overcoming
those limitations.

Neither of these figures is of course new in Rilke's
work. Of the difficulties attendant on the theme of the unrequited lover, *Die Aufzeichnungen* are eloquent, and it is
noticeable that Rilke's return to Gaspara Stampa in the
first Elegy is his last significant exploitation of the
motif - and with an apparent awareness that it contains no
further possibilities:

> ...Hast du der Gaspara Stampa
> denn genügend gedacht...? (EI,45)

As far as the dead are concerned, it is the early Eurydice
who represents Rilke's most complex attempt to exploit the
motif as symbol of a certain form of consciousness. That
attempt, it will be recalled, is structured around a
paradoxical combination of qualities - a closed self-
containment, answering to Rilke's anxieties concerning the
dissipation of the self, and a submissive 'Aufgelöstheit'
which answers to Rilke's impulse to experience self and
natural world, phenomenal and transcendental, as continuous.

These two qualities are both closely linked with the poem's
emphasis on her 'Gestorbensein'. In that light, two shifts
of emphasis are noticeable in the early Elegies. Firstly,
it is the 'Aufgelöstheit' of the young dead that is high-
lighted:

> das, was man war in unendlich ängstlichen Händen,
> nicht mehr zu sein, und selbst den eigenen Namen
> wegzulassen wie ein zerbrochenes Spielzeug.(EI,73)

The opposite quality is transposed into the brief mention of
the hero: 'es erhält sich der Held' (EI,41). Secondly, the
Elegy returns, as the earlier poem does not, from the dead
to the living. The passage describing the condition of the
dead is parenthetical, introduced by 'Freilich...', and
Rilke continues afterwards:

> ...Aber Lebendige machen
> alle den Fehler, daß sie zu stark unterscheiden.
> Engel (sagt man) wüßten oft nicht, ob sie unter
> Lebenden gehn oder Toten. (EI,80)

Eurydice's 'Gestorbensein' is brought into close association
with the insistence of Malte that life and death are but
one, and in the Elegy this association is seen as at least a
potential way forward. As F.D. Luke has put it, the 'after-
life' parable of the young dead in the first Elegy is an
'image of a breakthrough into a new way of seeing things, a
new way of being human. The spirits of the young dead are
the living - as they ought to be, but are not'.[73] And the
means by which the lesson of the dead could be learned by
the living forms the substance of the conclusion of the
Elegy. It is out of 'Trauer', that of the living for the
dead, that there may come 'seliger Fortschritt':

> Ist die Sage umsonst, daß einst in der Klage um
> Linos

wagende erste Musik dürre Erstarrung durchdrang;
daß erst im erschrockenen Raum, dem ein beinah
                                    göttlicher Jüngling
plötzlich für immer enttrat, das Leere in jene
Schwingung geriet, die uns jetzt hinreißt und
                          tröstet und hilft. (EI,91)

The note on which the first Elegy ends, though questioning,
could be described as hopeful. It leads away from the
absolute condition of the angels, but also away from
striving towards the absolute condition of the dead, towards
a life which incorporates so much of the 'other' as is
compatible with human existence. In so doing, it silently
by-passes the earlier clinging to an ideal of closed self-
containment.

   Not that the anxiety against which that ideal forms a
bulwark is bypassed; indeed, it forms the substance of the
second Elegy. The celebration of the angels as mirrors,
drawing their own beauty back into their own faces - a
paradoxical image of dynamic self-containment - is followed
immediately by lament for human dissipation:

        Denn wir, wo wir fühlen, verflüchtigen: ach wir
        atmen uns aus und dahin; von Holzglut zu Holzglut
        geben wir schwächern Geruch. (EII,18)

The theme is insistent; our being is dissolved into the
cosmos, we pass by 'wie ein luftiger Austausch', even our
experience of love, providing a momentary sense of being,
gives no 'Beweise'. The bulk of the Elegy reads as a
negative background to the celebration of 'Atmen, du
unsichtbares Gedicht', even to the imagery of breath and
cosmos. But it is neither towards despair nor towards *that*
form of celebration that the Elegy moves.

   For the second of the two directions in which these

early Elegies move away from their own initial premisses is set in a historical mode. Already the first Elegy had led to figures from the past; the second concludes with a more explicit contrast between ancient and modern in the evocation of 'die Vorsicht menschlicher Geste' on Attic stelae. The image of antiquity is of

> ...ein reines, verhaltenes, schmales
> Menschliches, einen unseren Streifen Fruchtlands
> zwischen Strom und Gestein. (EII,74)

It is an essentially *limited* ideal, dependent, insofar as Rilke's formulation 'Fänden auch wir...' permits him to see it as still potentially available, on a renunciation. The use of the word 'verhalten' echoes the initial renunciation of the cycle:

> Und so verhalt ich mich denn und verschlucke den
>   Lockruf
> dunkelen Schluchzens. (E II,8)

In this sense the conclusion of the second Elegy is comparable to that of the first, the image of music there - 'die uns jetzt hinreißt und tröstet und hilft' - being echoed here by the 'Bilder, die es besänftigen'.

But at the same time as Rilke sketched out these tentative directions in the first two Elegies, he was also sketching out the form of a conclusion to the whole cycle. Five lines, now the opening of the ninth Elegy, formulate a question: 'Warum denn Menschliches müssen?' The *content* of the answer was not to be supplied for ten years, but the *kind* of reply which Rilke felt to be required was dictated in advance - that is, in 1912 - by the three lines which now form the conclusion of that same Elegy:

> Siehe, ich lebe. Woraus? Weder Kindheit noch
> Zukunft
> werden weniger... Überzähliges Dasein
> entspringt mir im Herzen. (EIX,77)

In writing those lines, Rilke both undermined the
possibility of concluding the whole cycle in the way he
ended the first two Elegies, with a view of human
possibilities as 'verhalten' and 'schmal', and anticipated
a return to the earlier emphasis on the subsistence of the
self, a more comprehensive answer to the lament of the
second Elegy than that Elegy itself provided. Both these
aspects are in evidence also in the fragment later to
become, in a slightly modified form, the opening of the
tenth Elegy:

> Daß ich dereinst, an dem Ausgang der grimmigen
> Einsicht,
> Jubel und Ruhm aufsinge zustimmenden Engeln.
> Daß von den klar geschlagenen Hämmern des Herzens
> keiner versage an weichen, zweifelnden oder
> jähzornigen Saiten. Daß mich mein strömendes
> Antlitz
> glänzender mache... (II,64)

In this fragment, the basic 'hour-glass' shape of the cycle
is apparent; however strait the gate between lament and
affirmation, beyond it the dimensions are unlimited. Moreover, the emphasis is again shifted back from the 'submission' of the young dead to the 'Sich-Erhalten' of the
hero: 'Tumulte stürmisch entzückten Gefühls' are attributed,
in anticipation, to the poet as well as the angels.

Other fragments of the period, however, generally take
up the emphasis implied in the passage on the young dead.
The 'Streifen Fruchtlands' of the second Elegy is situated
'zwischen Strom und Gestein' - between, as Jacob Steiner
puts it, 'Dahinfließen' and 'Erstarrtsein'.[74] The first, as

has been shown, is lamented at length in the second Elegy in contrast to angelic 'Dasein'. The other, and opposite, danger inherent in the human condition is mentioned only tangentially in the passage devoted to the unrequited lover, with its lapidary formula: 'Denn Bleiben ist nirgends' (EI,53). But it is implied throughout as a negative background to the celebration of the young dead, who learn 'kaum erlernte Gebräuche nicht mehr zu üben...was man war in unendlich ängstlichen Händen,/nicht mehr zu sein' (EI,70). The theme is taken up again in the opening fragment of the ninth Elegy, comparing 'die Frist des Daseins' to the cycle of the laurel, where the main image suggests permanence, the interpolated metaphor ('wie eines Windes Lächeln'), transitoriness. In the fragment of the tenth, it is developed more fully, and associated with the insistence of the first Elegy that pain should become fruitful:

> ...Wir Vergeuder der Schmerzen.
> Wie wir sie absehn voraus in die traurige Dauer,
> ob sie nicht enden vielleicht. Sie aber sind ja
> Zeiten von uns, unser winter-
> währiges Laubwerk... (II,64)

Similarly, the opening lines of the sixth Elegy, written in January or February of 1913, emphasize the necessity of acceptance of the one 'season' which our common human consciousness would willingly ignore:

> Feigenbaum, seit wie lange schon ists mir
>   bedeutend,
> wie du die Blüte beinah ganz überschlägst
> und hinein in die zeitig entschlossene Frucht,
> ungerühmt, drängst dein reines Geheimnis.
>   ... Wir aber verweilen,
> ach, uns rühmt es zu blühn, und ins verspätete
>   Innre
> unserer endlichen Frucht gehn wir verraten hinein.
>   (EVI,1)

The theme is at least as old as *Das Buch von der Armut und vom Tode*. And indeed, there is little that is new in the Elegies of 1912 and 1913. Certain emphases are however important. Firstly, though the insistent anxieties concerning the self which marked Rilke's earlier work are broadened into universal lament in the second Elegy, the ideal of a closed self-sufficiency which had operated as defence against that anxiety is projected into the mythical Angels, defined as unavailable, and apparently, at first, renounced. Conversely, the quality of submissive 'Ausgelöstsein', long seen by Rilke as symbolic expression of an experience of self and natural world, transcendence and immanence, as continuous, comes to the fore in celebrations of death and the dead, which, however, unlike the situation in 'Orpheus. Eurydike. Hermes' are presented as quasi-ethical parables for the living rather than as imperative absolutes. Thirdly, the theme of dispossession which flows from that celebration of the dead hints at a more explicit awareness of the concept of 'self-containment' as precisely the major barrier to submission. Fourthly, however, Rilke's anticipatory conclusions to the cycle required of any new configuration of these elements that it permit a final closing of the circle, an emphasis on the subsistence of the self. The pattern adumbrated is that of a self preserved by its very dissolution, its subsistence assured by a paradoxical acceptance of its transitoriness so complete that it is absorbed into the natural order.

In 1913, however, the pattern was far from rounded and complete, and indeed, as will be argued, it is not completed in the Elegies. The major themes which dominate the fragmentary work of the next four years - the nature of that transcendental plane on which alone the paradox could be resolved, and the nature of that dispossession which is seen as precondition for the resolution - are both seen to be highly problematic. The first is explored most fully in the loosely grouped *Gedichte an die Nacht*, subjected recently to close critical scrutiny by Anthony Stephens, whose account is so full - and so revealing - that little is necessary here beyond a summary of his conclusions.[75]

The return to night as 'meeting-place of immanence and transcendence'[76] is reminiscent of *Das Buch vom mönchischen Leben*, and one of the circular configurations of that work - God as a projection of the 'Dunkelheit' within, which then enfolds and reconciles self and world - appears to recur in a poem such as 'Gedanken der Nacht...', in which the night as transcendental being is experienced as related to the immanent night within:

> Daß ihr *seid*, ist bejaht, daß hier, im gedrängten
> Behälter,
> Nacht, zu den Nächten hinzu, sich heimlich
> erzeugt.
> Plötzlich: mit welchem Gefühl, steht die unend-
> liche, älter,
> über die Schwester *in* mir, die ich berge, gebeugt.
> (II,68)

But, as Stephens points out, such an affirmative conclusion can only be seen as provisional, to the extent that it leaves out an area of problematic implied, but constantly elided, in the rapid dialectic of the *Stundenbuch*, that is, 'the question of whether the transcendent powers to which he addresses himself are an intensification and extension of something already innate in man or whether they represent something quite other and inaccessible'.[77] The concept of the younger sister in this poem is precisely an attempt to nuance the question to produce a satisfactory result, but the series as a whole does not sustain that procedure. In 'So angestrengt...', night is again seen as 'dieses ein-geborne Element', and linked therefore with the

'Sternenhimmel', permitting a more hopeful reworking of an elegiac motif:

> Vielleicht entziehts den Engeln etwas Kraft,
> daß nach uns her der Sternenhimmel nachgiebt...
> (II,52)

But the same poem transposes the indifference of the elegiac angels into the yet more distant 'Gods':

> Sie haben Dasein
> und nichts als Dasein, Überfluß von Dasein,
> doch nicht Geruch, nicht Wink. Nichts ist so
> stumm.
> wie eines Gottes Mund. (II,53)

In this context night appears as at best a mediator, and the series as a whole is, as Stephens says, inconclusive. It does however add a further mode of discourse to the other major theme of these years, that of 'dispossession'. Insofar as immanence and transcendence are here figured by proximity and distance, a range of vocabulary is made available which relates the two themes, as in 'Unwissend vor dem Himmel...' which, after questioning the relationship between self and stars, concludes:

> ...Abtun
> will ich die Wünsche, jeden andern Anschluß,
> mein Herz gewöhnen an sein Fernstes. Besser
> es lebt im Schrecken seiner Sterne, als
> zum Schein beschützt, von einer Näh beschwichtigt.
> (II,53)

This clearly relates to 'Seltsam, die Wünsche nicht weiter-zuwünschen' of the first Elegy. But the poem echoes the pattern of the parable of the young dead without using the image of death, and in so doing points towards a different development of the theme of dispossession. Three of the best known poems of the period are closely related to this development.

93

'Wendung', of July 1914, is one of the most frequently anthologized poems of these years. And yet it is a curiously unsatisfactory work. The use of the third person - 'Lange errang ers im Anschaun' - is uncharacteristic and uneasy, and although the poem speaks of a renunciation, the language used to describe the activities renounced betrays an air of complacency:

> Tiere traten getrost
> in den offenen Blick, weidende,
> und die gefangenen Löwen
> starrten hinein wie in unbegreifliche Freiheit...
> (II,82)

And the much quoted conclusion is marked by that empty abstraction - large words with little concrete content - which characterized so much of Rilke's verse before the *Neue Gedichte*:

> Denn des Anschauens, siehe, ist eine Grenze.
> Und die geschautere Welt
> will in der Liebe gedeihn.
>
> Werk des Gesichts ist getan,
> tue nun Herz-Werk
> an den Bildern in dir, jenen gefangenen...

As early as 1947, Dieter Bassermann pointed out the unsatisfactoriness of considering these formulae as marking a genuine watershed between *Neue Gedichte* and *Duineser Elegien* - the previously accepted interpretation - and subsequently the poem has been considered most commonly as belonging in the context of Rilke's personal crisis of the period, related principally to the brief 'Benvenuta' episode.[78] As Stephens has shown, however, Rilke's pre-occupation with the figure of 'die Geliebte' in this period is closely connected with other, less directly biographically inspired concerns;[79] and 'Wendung' can be seen, among

94

other things, as representing a not insignificant development of elegiac themes, especially when taken in conjunction
with 'Waldteich', the preceding poem in the *Sämtliche Werke*
and one which the drafts show to have been closely
associated with 'Wendung'.

'Waldteich' opens with a contrast similar to that of
'Die Rosenschale':

> Waldteich, weicher, in sich eingekehrter -,
> draußen ringt das ganze Meer und braust,
> aufgeregte Fernen drücken Schwerter
> jedem Sturmstoß in die Faust -,
> während du aus dunkler unversehrter
> Tiefe Spiele der Libellen schaust. (II,79f.)

The second stanza makes the parallels closer still, the
transforming power of the 'Innenräume' recalling the roses'
transformation of the whole phenomenal world into 'eine Hand
voll Innres':

> Was dort jenseits eingebeugter Bäume
> Überstürzung ist und Drang und Schwung,
> spiegelt sich in deine Innenräume
> als verhaltene Verdüsterung...

But the further development of the poem *questions* what is
implied in 'Die Rosenschale' - the equivalent power of the
poetic imagination:

> Wenn ich innig mich zusammenfaßte
> vor die unvereinlichsten Kontraste:
> weiter kam ich nicht: ich schaute an;
> blieb das Angeschaute sich entziehend...

If, indeed, the effort of 'Anschauen' is rewarded, the
victory is now seen as hollow:

95

schaut ich unbedingter, schaute knieend,
bis ich es in mich gewann.

Fand es in mir Liebe vor?
Tröstung für das aufgegebne Freie...

The victory would only be real if there were within the
poet's own self a 'space' akin to that of the 'Innenräume'
of the waters:

O hab ich keine Haine
in der Brust? kein Wehen? keine
Stille, atemleicht und frühlinglich?

Aware of the implied lack, the poet ends with plangent
lament:

Oh, ich habe zu der Welt kein Wesen,
wenn sich nicht da draußen die Erscheinung,
wie in leichter vorgefaßter Meinung,
weither heiter in mich freut.

It is these words, slightly altered, which become the
opening lines of the first draft of 'Wendung', become now
however not lament but *programme*:
Denn dies ist mein Wesen zur Welt...(II,417)
Disentangled from the purely private, the intuition sustaining 'Waldteich' and, more distantly, 'Wendung', is that the
divorce between human and natural is not to be overcome
through the detours of 'Die Rosenschale', but only by a
transformation of the inner self. The vocabulary of love,
with its imperatives, is principally, if not exclusively,
used for the reformulation of the quasi-ethical imperatives
implicit in the celebration of the young dead, or the
contrast of proximity and distance in the *Gedichte an die
Nacht*.

'Ausgesetzt auf den Bergen des Herzens' brings together

these three closely related strands. The image of the descent into death, leaving behind 'den eigenen Namen', of the first Elegy, is transposed here into an imagery of ascent, leaving behind 'die letzte Ortschaft der Worte' (II,94), while the 'Fernstes' of the night-poems, contrasted with the comfort of proximity, becomes the exposure on the 'Bergen des Herzens'. This basic image suggests the desire for an 'inner space' commensurate with the 'großgewohnten Dinge' of 'Waldteich', and a projected draft brings the poem into close relationship with 'Wendung':

> ausgesetzt. Plötzlich
> dennoch zu lieben. (II,424)

But Rilke abandoned this incongruous conclusion. And the most significant comparison between 'Wendung' and 'Ausgesetzt...' is to be found in the fact that the earlier poem suggests that the necessary 'Wendung', once its necessity is realized, is easily accomplished, whereas the later concludes:

> ...Aber
> ungeborgen, hier auf den Bergen des Herzens...

There is no assumption of desire for reality - only a terse suggestion of the triumph which might be plucked from this exposure, a suggestion contained in the verbal affinity of 'Berge' and 'bergen':

> ...und der große geborgene Vogel
> kreist um der Gipfel reine Verweigerung.

Again with the utmost economy, the poem suggests a resolution adumbrated, but not spelled out, in the 1912 Elegies:

        Da geht wohl, heilen Bewußtseins,
        manches umher, manches gesicherte Bergtier,
        wechselt und weilt.

The alliteration suggests a close association of transience
and permanence - an association explored at greater length
in the slightly early 'An Hölderlin', praising the addressee
for accepting the immutable law of change:

        die Zeile schloß sich wie Schicksal, ein Tod war
        selbst in der lindesten, und du betratest ihn;
                                                      aber
        der vorgehende Gott führte dich drüben hervor.
        O du wandelnder Geist, du wandelndster! (II,93)

        When Rilke returned to the Elegies in November 1915,
with the last significant poem to be written before silence
effectively fell for three years, it was with a similar
theme, modulated into the characteristic elegiac form of
universal lament:

        O Bäume Lebens, o wann winterlich?
        Wir sind nicht einig. Sind nicht wie die Zug-
        Vögel verständigt. Überholt und spät
        so drängen wir uns plötzlich Winden auf
        und fallen ein auf teilnahmslosen Teich. (EIV,1)

The Fourth Elegy takes to the utmost limits the image of
persistence associated with the dispossession theme of
'Ausgesetzt...' Like that poem, the central section of the
Elegy is an extended metaphor of the self; it is before
'seines Herzens Vorhang' that the poet sits:

        Der schlug sich auf. Die Szenerie war Abschied.
        Leicht zu verstehen. (EIV,20)

Set in the scenery of 'Dahinschwinden', our common human
lot, is the protagonist, the common human consciousness

rapidly dismissed as mere 'Bürger'. But the spectator sits
on:

> Wenn auch die Lampen ausgehn, wenn mir auch
> gesagt wird: Nichts mehr -, wenn auch von der
> Bühne
> das Leere herkommt mit dem grauen Luftzug...
> Ich bleibe dennoch. (EIV,30)

And his persistence is finally rewarded by an alternative
performance:

> ...wenn mir zumut ist,
> zu warten vor der Puppenbühne, nein,
> so völlig hinzuschauen, daß, um mein Schauen
> am Ende aufzuwiegen, dort als Spieler
> ein Engel hinmuß, der die Bälge hochreißt.
> Engel und Puppe: dann ist endlich Schauspiel.
> (EIV,52)

In this play of puppet and angel is resolved - apparently -
the dividedness of human consciousness and its alienation
from the total rhythm of the natural order:

> Dann kommt zusammen, was wir immerfort
> entzwein, indem wir da sind. Dann entsteht
> aus unsern Jahreszeiten erst der Umkreis
> des ganzen Wandelns. (EIV,58)

But the persistence of the spectator, his expectation
that this persistence will *oblige* the angel to intervene,
recalls the persistence of the prodigal in waiting for God
to requite his love, and the persistent 'Anschauen' of
'Waldteich'. And it is impossible to see the alternative
'performance' of the fourth Elegy as any less problematical
than the 'results' of those earlier forms of persistence.
More than any other single feature, it is the sharp, if
desperate *irony* of this poem which marks Rilke's re-entry
into the world of the Elegies. It is by no means fortuitous

that the entire episode is presented with a child-like
voice, from the intransigent 'Nicht *der*', the appealing
'Hab ich nicht recht!', the wilful 'wenn mir zumut ist' to
the satisfied 'Dann ist endlich Schauspiel'. And when the
child-like voice is dropped for the plangency of the central
elegiac voice, the theme announced is that of nostalgia *for*
childhood,

> die seit Anbeginn
> gegründet war für einen reinen Vorgang. (EIV,74)

What satisfies the child-like voice of the central section
is not necessarily available to the adult voice which
laments, and would not necessarily satisfy.

The Elegy thus draws to a close not triumphant, but
striking in its combination of nostalgia and grotesqueness:

> ...Wer macht den Kindertod
> aus grauem Brot, das hart wird, - oder läßt
> ihn drin im runden Mund, so wie den Gröps
> von einem schönen Apfel?... Mörder sind
> leicht einzusehen. Aber dies: den Tod,
> den ganzen Tod, noch *vor* dem Leben so
> sanft zu enthalten und nicht bös zu sein,
> ist unbeschreiblich. (EIV,78)

Only one poem in the whole of Rilke's work is perhaps
comparable in its bitterness:

> Da steht der Tod, ein bläulicher Absud
> in einer Tasse ohne Untersatz. (II,103)

The poem is nearly contemporary with the fourth Elegy, and
develops the theme of human unwillingness to submit to pain
and death into an impatient, despairing and grotesque
indictment:

Man muß ihnen die harte Gegenwart
ausnehmen, wie ein künstliches Gebiß.
Dann lallen sie. Gelall, Gelall...
....

This is the note on which Rilke virtually ceased writing in
November of 1915. The Elegies were unfinished, and the gap
between the conclusions of the first two and the promise of
the fragments of the ninth and tenth unbridged. No more
than in *Die Aufzeichnungen* had Rilke found a resolution of
the tensions which had come to the surface in that work; the
principal theme emerging from the early Elegies, that of
'dispossession', was left at this point of ironic despair.

       *   *   *   *   *   *   *   *

To turn from the fourth Elegy and 'Der Tod' to the
verses Rilke started writing after the war is to witness an
astonishing transformation. Take, for instance, the sonnet
of November 1919:

> O wenn ein Herz, längst wohnend im Entwöhnen,
> von aller Kunft und Zuversicht getrennt,
> erwacht und plötzlich hört, wie man es nennt:
> 'Du Überfluß, Du Fülle alles Schönen!' (II,237)

The example is by no means isolated; this note is dominant
in the following months. In February of 1920 he writes:

> Letztes ist nicht, daß man sich überwinde
> nur daß man still aus solcher Mitte liebt,
> daß man auch noch um Not und Zorn das Linde,
> Zärtliche fühlt, das uns zuletzt umgiebt. (II,242)

A radical transformation of Rilke's personal experience
is recorded in these small occasional verses. How it came
about is not a question that need delay us here; and indeed,
Rilke recorded his own astonishment in the earlier of the
two poems quoted:

> Hier tönt ein Herz, das sich im Gram verschwieg,
> und zweifelt, ob ihm dies zu Recht gebühre:
> so reich zu sein in seiner Armut Sieg.

The contrast between pre-war 'Gram' and post-war 'Sieg' is
indeed striking, but it is significant that the latter *is*
expressed in small occasional verses. The cycle *Aus dem
Nachlaß des Grafen C.W.* presents the most interesting case
in this respect. The opening poem of the second series
expresses that same sense of surprise, gratitude and
humility:

> Dies wird einmal der Sommer sein.
> Eine vollendete Wohnung.
> Welches Gedräng an der Tür!
> Alles zieht selig ein.
> Wie zur Belohnung.
> Wofür? (II,123)

There is presumably no need to delay on the mysterious
'Count C.W.' to whom Rilke claimed to have served as mere
secretary. But, as Bassermann has pointed out, the fact
that Rilke felt it necessary on this occasion to use a
pseudonym is in itself significant.[80] Significant, that is,
of a sense that while the Elegies were still uncompleted, the
feelings expressed by these verses were in some sense
'unjustified'. If this new experience of life were to form
part of the affirmative climax which the Elegies required,
it would have to be brought into the existing dramatic
structure and set against the weight of lament in the existing Elegies.

The seventh Elegy - first of the 1922 Elegies after the
discarded *Gegen-Strophen* - is partly an attempt to achieve
that integration. The sixth of the second series of *Aus dem
Nachlaß...* offers some reflections on the nature of the
transformation Rilke felt he had undergone:

> Gekonnt hats keiner; denn das Leben währt
> weils keiner konnte. Aber der Versuche
> Unendlichkeit!...
> Weils keiner meistert, bleibt das Leben rein.
> Ists nicht verlegne Kraft wenn ich am Morgen
> turne? (II,126)

The general sense here - of a continuity of life preserved
despite active effort - is taken up in the opening of the
seventh Elegy:

> Werbung nicht mehr, nicht Werbung, entwachsene
> Stimme,
> sei deines Schreies Natur...

The renunciation of 'Werbung' here answers, within the
dramatic framework of the Elegies, to the opening of the
first Elegy, but the hypothetical cry which follows is no
'Lockruf dunkelen Schluchzens'. E.L. Stahl, in his commentary on this passage, notes Rilke's conviction 'that desire
and longing, even in love, are divisive emotions', and
argues that it is on these grounds that he is renouncing
'Werbung'.[81] But in a sense, it is *not* renounced; it is
simply dismissed as *superfluous*. In the condition of
'Entwachsenheit' postulated in the first line, there would
be nothing limited or divisive about the poet's cry; it
would be as pure as the cry of the bird, as the 'Ton der
Verkündigung' which is that of the entire natural world.
The entire passage which follows derives unmistakably from
the atmosphere of the short occasional poems of the period,
its mounting exuberance witnessing to Rilke's overwhelming
sense of existential salvation:

> Nicht nur die Morgen alle des Sommers -, nicht nur
> wie sie sich wandeln in Tag und strahlen vor
> Anfang.
> Nicht nur die Tage, die zart sind um Blumen, und
> oben,
> um die gestalteten Bäume, stark und gewaltig.

103

Nicht nur die Andacht dieser entfalteten Kräfte,
nicht nur die Wege, nicht nur die Wiesen im Abend,
nicht nur, nach spätem Gewitter, das atmende
                                                Klarsein,
nicht nur der nahende Schlaf und ein Ahnen,
                                    abends... (EVII,22)

But the passage needed to be drawn into the dramatic
framework; the mere *announcement* of an upsurge of vital
energy would not suffice for a cycle of such an argumentative nature, which had asked 'Habt ihr Beweise?' And so
the Elegy modulates subtly back into that framework, firstly
by the conclusion of the 'nicht nur' series in images of
night and death, and secondly by the call to lovers - those
of whom the question had been asked. Further, if the cry of
the poet is unlimited, it would not exclude the dead, but
would call back to life 'die Versunkenen' - a reversal of the
Orpheus/Eurydice situation. The sophistry is clearly a
device for placing the triumphant note of the earlier part of
the Elegy back into relationship with the 'negative' themes.
What emerges from that confrontation is akin to the conclusion of the first two Elegies: a recognition of the human,
freed from the all-too-human, a consciousness which has
learned the lesson of the dead within the limitations of
mortal life:

                    ...Ihr Kinder, ein hiesig
        einmal ergriffenes Ding gälte für viele...
        Hiersein ist herrlich. (EVII,34)

The link between the second and the seventh Elegies
becomes closer as a further modulation takes the latter
into a historical mode. Just as the possibilities of 'einen
unseren Streifen Fruchtlands' were perceived in the first
instance in the past, so now the present is seen as a time
which threatens those possibilities. The fifth section of
the seventh develops powerfully what the second had implied
nostalgically:

> ...und wir können ihm nicht mehr
> nachschauen in Bilder, die es besänftigen...
> (EII,77)
>   ...Und immer geringer
> schwindet das Außen. Wo einmal ein dauerndes Haus
>   war,
> schlägt sich erdachtes Gebild vor...(EVII,51)

But the seventh Elegy, unlike the second, does not close at
that point:

> ...Diese, des Herzens, Verschwendung,
> sparen wir heimlicher ein. Ja, wo noch eins
>   übersteht,
> ein einst gebetetes Ding, ein gedientes,
>   geknietes -,
> hält es sich, so wie es ist, schon ins Unsicht-
>   bare hin.
> Viele gewahrens nicht mehr, doch ohne den Vorteil,
> daß sie's nun *innerlich* baun, mit Pfeilern und
>   Statuen, größer! (EVII,57)

The outer forms which in earlier ages gave shape to human
experience are disappearing, becoming invisible - if we are
to continue to shape our experience, it will be invisibly,
within. The poet, so to speak, over-trumps the historical
process, to make advantage out of disadvantage. And though
the task will be carried on in a different manner, it
remains the same task - to preserve, despite the pressures
of the age, the shape of the human.

   A series of *Duineser Elegien* could perhaps be made out
of the first, second and seventh; it would be lesser in
scope than the complete cycle, but more internally consistent. Following a pattern of lament for the human condition
in comparison with the angelic, as a mythic precipitate of
undivided consciousness and unmenaced self-subsistence, it
would renounce striving for that condition, would learn
what was to be learned by way of submission from the dead,
and find consolation and vindication in the affirmation of

what humanity has nevertheless achieved on its own terms, and in determination to preserve and extend that achievement in an unpropitious time. When the poet, at the end of the seventh Elegy, turns challengingly to the Angel, it is with a repeated emphasis on 'wir' - we humans who, despite our mortal and divided condition, have achieved something which is 'ours':

> War es nicht Wunder? O staune, Engel, denn *wir*
>   sinds,
> wir, o du Großer, erzähls...
>   So haben wir dennoch
> nicht die Räume versäumt, diese gewährenden, diese
> *unseren* Räume. (EVII,75)

But despite the note of triumph, there was something modest about such conclusions - 'verhaltenes, schmales', in Rilke's own words. And from the outset, in the anticipatory fragments of the ninth and tenth, he had imagined a conclusion of a less limited, less conditional kind. Subsequently, especially in the fourth Elegy, he had deepened lament to a point of despair against which the conclusion of the seventh seemed incommensurate, calling into question so radically what *was* the human that the injunction to preserve the human could not be a final answer.

And so the eighth Elegy plunges back into lament. And not simply into lament - for it would be difficult to see how the dramatic tension of the whole cycle could be sustained if there were not at this point some 'recul pour mieux sauter' - but into the kind of lament which seems to ignore the triumph of the seventh. In the consistency of its lament, in the heavy iambic rhythm which predominates - as it does also in the fourth - it is perhaps the most unified in tone of all the Elegies, exploring and deepening the contrast of the opening lines of the fourth:

O Bäume Lebens, o wann winterlich?
Wir sind nicht einig. Sind nicht wie die Zug-
Vögel verständigt. (EIV,1)

Mit allen Augen sieht die Kreatur
das Offene. Nur unsre Augen sind
wie umgekehrt und ganz um sie gestellt
als Fallen, rings um ihren freien Ausgang.(EVIII,1)

Against the possibility of a narrow human arena, incorporat-
ing an awareness of death, Rilke now implicitly demands a
condition of life so lacking in awareness of distinction
between life and death as to be 'frei von Tod'. Seen
against this demand, the alienation of man from the rhythms
and unity of the natural order acquires the quality of an
unbridgeable chasm:

Dieses heißt Schicksal: gegenüber sein
und nichts als das und immer gegenüber. (EVIII,33)

Und wir: Zuschauer, immer, überall,
dem allen zugewandt und nie hinaus! (EVIII,66)

Just as the use of the puppet-symbol in the fourth
Elegy lends an ironic edge to the child's demands for a more
'satisfactory' performance, so here the search for a
condition of life not marked by dividedness of consciousness
leads beyond the child, beyond even the 'wachsam warmen
Tier' to the ironic hyperbole of

O Seligkeit der *kleinen* Kreatur,
die immer *bleibt* im Schoße, der sie austrug;
O Glück der Mücke, die noch *innen* hüpft,
selbst wenn sie Hochzeit hat: denn Schooß ist
                                    Alles. (EVIII,52)

And the parallels with the fourth Elegy continue to the
conclusion, in which the former's 'Szenerie des Abschieds'
is echoed by

so leben wir und nehmen immer Abschied. (EVIII,75)

This conclusion leads, with admirable economy of means, into the opening of the ninth Elegy, extant from 1912, and to the point where an answer had finally to be given to the ten-year-old question: 'warum denn Menschliches müssen?' The announcement 'Aber weil Hiersein viel ist' immediately recalls the 'Hiersein ist herrlich' of the seventh Elegy, though the proviso 'Oh, *nicht*, weil Glück *ist*' seems to undercut certain aspects of the earlier Elegy. On a superficial reading, the curve of the ninth follows closely that of the seventh. There is the same emphasis on the present time as a 'dumpfe Umkehr der Welt':

> ...Mehr als je
> fallen die Dinge dahin, die erlebbaren, denn,
> was sie verdrängend ersetzt, ist ein Tun ohne Bild.
> (EIX,44)

There is the same emphasis on the preservation of the shape of the human experience. Indeed, as Stahl notes, the task is more modestly described in the ninth than in the seventh, in the sense that human feelings are to be preserved not in 'Chartres' and 'music', but in

> Haus,
> Brücke, Brunnen, Tor, Krug, Obstbaum, Fenster, -
> höchstens: Säule, Turm... (EIX,32)

in other words, in simple artefacts, and in objects of the natural world which have become repositories of the human through secular usage:

> das Einfache, das, von Geschlecht zu
> Geschlechtern gestaltet,
> als ein Unsriges lebt... (EIX,56)

Despite these similarities, however, the ninth Elegy goes beyond the seventh in two significant ways. Firstly,

in the seventh Elegy there is no discussion of the status
attached to the task prescribed; it is a self-evident human
imperative:

> ...*Uns* soll
> dies nicht verwirren; es stärke in uns die
> Bewahrung
> der noch erkannten Gestalt. (EVII,65)

In the ninth, however, it is enjoined

> ...weil uns scheinbar
> alles das Hiesige braucht, dieses Schwindende, das
> seltsam uns angeht. (EIX,11)

The theme relates to the intuition of the first Elegy that
the natural world in some sense 'uns angeht'. The sense of
'Auftrag' there however appears to be parallel to the
general sense of the 'Was sie mir wollen?' of the
section on 'voices', or the '*könnten* wir sein/ohne sie?' of
the passage on the young dead. In each of these cases the
poet urges that we have something to *learn* from each of
these - from the natural world as from the silence and from
the dead - as he had urged years before:

> Vor lauter Lauschen und Staunen sei still,
> du mein tieftiefes Leben;
> daß du weißt, was der Wind dir will,
> eh noch die Birken beben. (I,154)

The ninth Elegy, on the other hand, echoes the later part of
that early poem:

> Und dann meine Seele sei weit, sei weit,
> daß dir das Leben gelinge,
> breite dich wie ein Feierkleid
> über die sinnenden Dinge.

In other words, the sense that we have to learn from natural
objects is reversed in the prescription of a specific task
which will be our vindication and salvation; to be human is

defined *by* that task: 'Sind wir vielleicht *hier*, um zu
sagen...?', and indeed,

> zu *sagen*, verstehs,
> oh zu sagen *so*, wie selber die Dinge niemals
> innig meinten zu sein. (EIX,34)

And the sense attached to this task in the seventh Elegy,
that of the celebration of *artefacts* as repositories of the
human, is elided into the celebration of the natural world,
an elision effected by the use of the word 'Ding', so that
from 'Haus, Brücke, Brunnen...', the Elegy moves into 'Die
heimliche List/dieser verschwiegenen Erde'. In its first
appearance the sense is ambiguous, for the Elegy returns
to 'die Schwelle' as locus of continuity between
generations. But in the succeeding passage, with the
injunction to demonstrate to the Angel the range of human
achievement, Rilke's design is clear. First indeed comes
the injunction to show him 'das Einfache', 'das Unsrige',
but then, with 'Sag ihm die Dinge', Rilke proceeds to sub-
sume under that heading first the art-work -

> wie selbst das klagende Leid rein zur Gestalt sich
> entschließt,
> dient als ein Ding, oder stirbt in ein Ding -, und
> jenseits
> selig der Geige entgeht.

- and then natural objects, not, like 'Obstbaum', as
adoptively human objects, but as elements of the natural
order:

> Erde, ist es nicht dies, was du willst:
> *unsichtbar*
> in uns erstehn? - Ist es dein Traum nicht,
> einmal unsichtbar zu sein? - Erde! unsichtbar!
> Was, wenn Verwandlung nicht, ist dein drängender
> Auftrag?
> Erde, du liebe, ich will. (EIX,68)

The use of terms such as 'Ding' and 'Erde' in this abstract manner is in itself a throwback to a much earlier manner, as if ignoring all that had come between. The questioning of the previous ten years is not so much answered as brushed aside in the attribution to the earth of a desire to re-arise in the divided, lamented human consciousness. Across the years, the circular tactic of the ninth Elegy - imputing to 'die Erde' a desire which reflects human anxiety, and resolving that anxiety *by* imputing it to the greater reality - echoes nothing in Rilke's earlier work so directly as it does *Mir zur Feier*:

> Alle Angst ist nur ein Anbeginn,
> aber ohne Ende ist die Erde,
> und das Bangen ist nur die Gebärde,
> und die Sehnsucht ist ihr Sinn. (I,155)

And, as in that early poem, the result is not a resolution, but an evasive exorcism, of lament.

The ninth Elegy changes the emphases of the seventh in another, related manner. The seventh, as remarked earlier, had clear affinities with the first and second in its ideal of 'ein reines, verhaltenes, schmales/Menschliches'. The ninth modulates this theme into a different tonality:

> Zwischen den Hämmern besteht
> unser Herz, wie die Zunge
> zwischen den Zähnen... (EIX,49)

Despite the emphatic '*Ein* Mal' of the second section, a more radically intransigent note is in evidence: 'Am liebsten/ alles behalten für immer...' This note comes to the fore when the 1922 section of the Elegy comes to a close with

> Immer warst du im Recht, und dein heiliger Einfall
> ist der vertrauliche Tod. (EIX,76)

This emphasis on death leads again away from the moderate
conclusions of the 1912 Elegies, as is strikingly
illustrated by the amendment Rilke made in 1922 to the
opening passage of the tenth Elegy. In the 1913 version,
pain was described as

        Zeiten von uns, unser winter-
        währiges Laubwerk, Wiesen, Teiche,
                    angeborene Landschaft... (II,64)
In 1922 this was intensified by

                                    ... nicht nur
        Zeit -, sind Stelle, Siedelung, Lager, Boden,
                            Wohnort. (EX,14)

The emphasis laid here on the one season of pain and death
links the tenth Elegy, in its final form, with the bitter
indictment of 'Der Tod' of 1915; and the first half of the
Elegy represents a development of Rilke's painful awareness
of our tendency to ignore that season into a powerful
denunciation, especially in the excoriation of the 'Trost-
markt' and the 'Plakaten des "Todlos"',

        jenes bitteren Biers, das den Trinkenden süß
                                            scheint,
        wenn sie immer dazu frische Zerstreuungen kaun...
                                        (EX,36)

    The journey of the young dead through the 'weite Land-
schaft der Klagen' recalls the first Elegy's parable, but
intensified and subtly altered. The passage in the first
Elegy concludes:

                            ...Aber Lebendige machen
        alle den Fehler, daß sie zu stark unterscheiden.
                                        (EI,80)

In the sharp contrast of the 'Gassen der Leid-Stadt' and the
'Landschaft der Klagen', Rilke does not so much redress the

balance as swing the pendulum to the other extreme. Stahl
notes the parallel between the 'Quelle der Freude' which
rises in the mountains of the 'Leidland' to be 'bei den
Menschen...ein tragender Strom' (EX,100) and the conviction
expressed in the first Elegy that 'we, the living, derive
comfort and help from those who have departed into death'.[83]
But in the first Elegy the consolation is mediate, and the
living are implicitly enjoined to learn while living the
lesson the dead have to offer. In the tenth, the
consolatory message brought by the stream appears, as
L.G. Salingar has said of the consolatory message from the
dead in Eliot's *Little Gidding*, 'to come to no more than
that they *are* dead'.[84] 'La vraie vie est ailleurs', and the
living youth momentarily moved by the beauty of 'eine junge
Klage' to venture beyond the 'Gassen der Leid-Stadt' quickly
returns; no lesson is learned by the living, nor is any real
indication given of how they might learn.

> Nur die jungen Toten, im ersten Zustand
> zeitlosen Gleichmuts, dem der Entwöhnung,
> folgen ihr liebend. (EX,47)

The situation is an exact reversal of that of Eurydice, but
it carries the same intransigent aspiration for an absolute
condition, with all mediation refused.

And finally the tenth Elegy leads, not into 'einen
unseren Streifen Fruchtlands', but into

> die Berge des Ur-leids.
> Und nicht einmal sein Schritt klingt aus dem
> tonlosen Los. (EX,104)

*   *   *   *   *   *   *   *

E.L. Stahl, among other recent critics, has noted the
fact that the *Duineser Elegien* have been subject to praise or
blame on the grounds of their supposed metaphysical doctrines,

and has argued that both approval and disapproval of this nature stem from a misconception of the nature of poetic discourse.[85] Because of the prevalence in earlier works of criticism of 'misconceptions' of this variety, recent commentators - where they have not been sweepingly dismissive of Rilke's work as a whole - have tended to be wary of any kind of 'approval' or 'disapproval'. Jacob Steiner's commentary bears monumental witness to the conviction that the Elegies represent a totally consistent, autonomous poetic world,[86] and Stahl himself argues that 'the criterion of soundness can only be applied to the argument when its poetic function ceases to be the centre of attention'.[87] The notion of 'poetic function', however, is far from self-explanatory, and doubts of one kind or another continue to be expressed, as, to take but one example, in Käte Hamburger's characterization of the ninth Elegy as a form of 'transzendentaler Extremismus'.[88]

Certainly, to disagree with the 'statements' made by a poem, to dismiss a poetic argument because it is an apparent affront to common sense - as is often the case with the commentary of Romano Guardini[89] - is to be guilty of that 'critical primitivism', in F.D. Luke's phrase, which does not recognize the indirections of literary discourse.[90] But the 'poetic function', in the case of the ninth and tenth Elegies, has to be defined in terms of their role in the cycle as a whole, and in a more general sense, in terms of their relationship to the tensions and questioning of the preceding years. And in this light two comments are not only permissible, but mandatory.

Firstly, the total 'statement' made by the cycle, through its various forms of metaphor and indirection, is not self-consistent. The Elegies are akin to Goethe's *Faust* in the sense that the first, second and seventh form

a kind of *Urfaust* (though not in a chronological sense)
which is overlaid with a more ambitious and wide-ranging
'plot'. The transition from one to the other is masked by
the superficial parallelism of the seventh and ninth, and
effected through something akin to verbal sleight-of-hand,
in the elision of different areas of explicit and implicit
meaning attached to the word 'Ding'. In a more general
sense, the resulting affirmative conclusion is presented as
if it cancelled out all previous lament and questioning,
with nothing to indicate to the reader why this should be
so.

Secondly, seen in the light of Rilke's total work
previous to 1922, it is far from clear that the two final
Elegies are consistent with each other. If the fundamental
problematic of Rilke's work is defined, in Käte Hamburger's
terms, as 'die Frage nach dem Anteil des Ich an dem was
"ist"',[91] two major directions towards a resolution of that
problematic can be defined. One takes the form of a lesson
to be learned, that of 'submission', associated most
commonly with the metaphor of death. The other is a claim
to a creative, transforming power within the self, figured
in a variety of images - rose-bowl, statue, woodland lake,
Angel. From the earliest work, Rilke strives to effect a
link between the two, from the simple juxtapositions of 'Vor
lauter Lauschen' to the complex paradoxes and nuances of the
Neue Gedichte and *Die Aufzeichnungen*. In the period
immediately preceding the conclusion of the Elegies, the
central intuition sustaining Rilke's work is that submission
is the *precondition* of creative power. In the final
Elegies, Rilke relapses, in effect, into juxtaposition. The
ninth Elegy, bypassing that intuition, appeals in its
implied claim of a teleologically assured relationship with
'die Erde' to a source of creative transformation within the
self. The tenth, brushing aside the mediate, indicative

conclusions of earlier Elegies, places 'die Quelle der Freude' in the landscape of death. Despite some 'cross-reference', there is little real connexion between the two.

It has been often enough pointed out that Rilke himself was responsible for encouraging 'misconceptions' about the Elegies, for encouraging, that is, a 'metaphysical' reading, notably in his letter to his Polish translator Hulewicz. But Rilke's reading cannot be simply dismissed by reference to the 'intentional fallacy'. For it is only *through* such a metaphysical 'system' as Rilke there elaborates that the ninth and tenth Elegies can be harmonized. At the level of 'poetic function' - that is to say, as expressive of certain anxieties and aspirations, interpreted in the total context of Rilke's own work - the final Elegies represent not a resolution but, like *Das Buch vom mönchischen Leben*, a precarious point of balance.

There is a sense in which recognition of that fact is built into the elegiac structure itself. One marked feature of all earlier Elegies, their ironic awareness of possible ambiguity, is absent from either the perfervid celebration of the ninth, or the mingled recrimination and sentimentality of the tenth. It returns in full force in the fifth - apart from a few finishing touches to the seventh, last in order of composition. If one suspects some kind of verbal acrobatics in the ninth Elegy, then the image of the fifth is not adventitiously chosen. The reader's reaction to the extraordinary leap which takes the cycle from lament to triumph might well be figured in the lines:

> Und plötzlich in diesem mühsamen Nirgends,
> plötzlich
> die unsägliche Stelle, wo sich das reine Zuwenig
> unbegreiflich verwandelt -, umspringt
> in jenes leere Zuviel. (EV,81)

116

And if achievement is cast in doubt, with the transposition
into a hopeful subjunctive of a genuinely successful
'performance', what is meantime unambiguously salvaged is
that 'reine Zuwenig', the *Subrisio Saltat*, symbol of

>   der Ort - ich trag ihn im Herzen -,
>   wo sie noch lange nicht *konnten*... (EV,73)

Which recalls that poem *Aus dem Nachlaß*...:

>   Gekonnt hats keiner; denn das Leben währt
>   weils keiner konnte. Aber der Versuche
>   Unendlichkeit! (II,126)

Which in turn leads one to the 'epilogue' to the elegiac
cycle:

>   Und wir, die an *steigendes* Glück
>   denken, empfänden die Rührung,
>   die uns beinah bestürzt,
>   wenn ein Glückliches *fällt*. (EX,110)

The Elegies retain, beyond the 'conclusions' of ninth and
tenth, their exploratory, ironic, self-cancelling character,
pointing as they end to other possibilities - possibilities
already being explored in the contemporary *Sonette an
Orpheus*.

VI. THE EXAMPLE OF VALERY

La Jeune Parque, Odes, Note et digression,
'Le Cimetière marin', *L'Ame et la danse*

A cry, no less problematical than that which announces
the *Duineser Elegien*, opens *La Jeune Parque*:

> Qui pleure là, sinon le vent simple, à cette heure
> Seule, avec diamants extrêmes?...Mais qui pleure,
> Si proche de moi-même au moment de pleurer?

The question appears to answer itself in the word 'seule'.
But at the same time it is not answered, for the self which
cries is not the self which asks the question:

> Cette main, sur mes traits qu'elle rêve effleurer,
> Distraitement docile à quelque fin profonde,
> Attend de ma faiblesse une larme qui fonde,
> Et que de mes destins lentement divisé,
> Le plus pur en silence éclaire un coeur brisé. (4)

Valéry returns here to the first-person lyric form of
'Narcisse parle', and Narcissus himself is recalled in the
attentiveness to an inner condition and in the tear itself.
But this protagonist is aware of an equivocation within the
self foreign to the gentle melancholy of the earlier poem.

Then again, the hypothesis that it is the wind that
cries is dismissed and is not dismissed. For the
distinction between self and world is blurred in the

118

heroine's awakening: those 'diamants extrêmes' which are her
sole companions may be the distant stars, or her tears themselves, the brilliant distillation of her emotional
extremity. Like Valéry's early Venus born from the waves,
the Fate only slowly distinguishes herself from the chaos of
night; the wind cries with her, the swell carries her own
self-reproach, and the very strangeness of the stars is an
intimacy:

> Je scintille, liée à ce ciel inconnu...
> L'immense grappe brille à ma soif de désastres.
>
> (16)

Mysterious to herself as to the reader, she wavers between
seeing herself as whole and as divided, as linked to the
world around and as detached from it.

> La Jeune Parque, writes Jean Hytier,
> ...occupe une position centrale dans l'oeuvre de Paul
> Valéry. Bien qu'écrite vingt ans après les poèmes de
> la Conque, elle achève l'Album de vers anciens et elle
> prélude au recueil de Charmes.[92]

Up to a certain point - a point which will be defined later
- La Jeune Parque can be seen as the dialectic which ensues
from the re-integration into a single persona of the
rigorously separated inhabitants of the Album - of the
'porosity' of the second or third-person protagonists with
the observant detachment of the poet's own voice. 'Sens
universel, et spécifiquement valéryen' is Marcel Raymond's
characterization of the poem's import:

> ...la Jeune Parque est partagée, une double tentation
> l'assaille, celle de la conscience négative - volonté
> implacable de lucidité, de pureté, qui fait que tout
> lui devient étranger - et tentation de la vie, ou de
> la volonté de vivre, qui est opposée à la
> conscience...[93]

Part of the difference between the *Album* and the *Jeune
Parque* - the intensification of a rather langorous fin-de-
siècle figure of self-absorption into a self-conscious and
passionate will to self-sufficient purity - is due to the
intervention of Teste. But the opening lines of the poem
could hardly be imagined as coming from the mouth of the
'homme de verre'; his nostalgia for an uncontaminated
reality is caught up with the 'porosity' of the earlier
protagonists and intensified into an overwhelming urge for
reabsorption into a world of vital energy. The concluding
lines of the first section, down to details of vocabulary,
are part Narcissus, part Teste, but the sense of both menace
and power exceeds anything found in either:

> ...Ou si le mal me suit d'un songe refermé,
> Quand (au velours du souffle envolé l'or des
> lampes)
> J'ai de mes bras épais environné mes tempes,
> Et longtemps de mon âme attendu les éclairs?
> Toute? Mais toute à moi, maîtresse de mes chairs,
> Durcissant d'un frisson leur étrange étendue,
> Et dans mes doux liens, à mon sang suspendue,
> Je me voyais me voir, sinueuse, et dorais
> De regards en regards, mes profondes forêts. (28)

'Double tentation', according to Raymond. A temptation implies a condition preceding the temptation.
M. Teste is presented to the reader only at a point where
he has travelled far along his particular road, and his
previous condition can only be conceived of as 'normality'.
But the young Fate (despite her semi-mythological status)
is, in a sense, a more human figure than Teste (despite his
outward status as Parisian *rentier* of the 1890s); in her case
the temptation itself and the ensuing drama are to be
thought of as 'normal', as universal, the fate - this is
certainly one meaning of the poem's title - of all humanity.
Her 'Eden' is thus to be defined in other terms, and her own
definition is in terms of *harmony* - harmony within her own
self:

> Femme flexible et ferme aux silences suivis
> D'actes purs! (103)

harmony with her body:

> Vers mes sens lumineux nageait ma blonde argile
> (138)

and harmony with the world about her:

> ... J'étais l'égale et l'épouse du jour,
> Seul support souriant que je formais d'amour
> A la toute-puissante altitude adorée... (107)

But this Eden is not situated at the beginning of the poem, nor even, in any real sense, at any chronologically definable point in the Fate's life. One cannot simply restore a straightforward sequence to Valéry's 'narrative' by altering the sequence of the sections. 'Conscience signifie d'abord mémoire': it is through the heroine's grappling with her memories that the drama unfolds, and those 'memories' are partly constructs of her 'present' state. In the second section, under the guise of following the serpent's activities, the Fate turns her attention to the alienation she senses within herself, and constructs a linear narrative of harmony followed by disturbance. In defining her previous condition as that of

> ...une vierge à soi-même enlacée,
> Jalouse... (45)

the final word betrays that the description is itself a reaction to her present condition. The passage continues:

> ... Mais de qui, jalouse et menacée?
> Et quel silence parle à mon seul possesseur?
>
> Dieux! Dans ma lourde plaie une secrète soeur
> Brûle, qui se préfère à l'extrême attentive. (46)

Construction of a linear narrative is followed by a casting of dramatic roles, between a 'secrète soeur', sensitive to

the serpent's bite, and a self defined as 'l'extrême
attentive', observant, jealous and defensive. The casting
of roles is itself followed by the definition of relationships between them. Finding the source of her temptation
within herself, the Fate prides herself on her ability to
do without the serpent, on her clear perception of the
workings of the 'secrète soeur' of sensibility, and sets up
one part of her multiple self as guardian of the rest:

> Je m'accoude inquiète et pourtant souveraine,
> Tant de mes visions parmi la nuit et l'oeil,
> Les moindres mouvements consultent mon orgueil.
>
> (94)

But the balance is unstable, and the whole of the first
half of the poem is structured around a dialectical
intensification of self-alienation, each temporary point of
rest being overtaken by further internal conflict resulting
in ever more rigid divisions within the self. Twice the
Fate calls on the Eden of her 'memory', but in retrospect,
premonitions of alienation are found even there, in the
shadow which slipped 'entre la rose et moi'. The
recognition is an advance both in self-knowledge and in
self-alienation, for in returning to her 'present' state,
she sees herself as irremediably divided and alienated from
the world around, but at the same time armed by her
knowledge:

> Et moi vive, debout,
> Dure, et de mon néant secrètement armée,
> Mais, comme par l'amour une joue enflammée,
> Et la narine jointe au vent de l'oranger,
> Je ne rends plus au jour qu'un regard étranger...
>
> (148)

In the second recollection, the only part of her former life
which speaks to her is a premonition of sexual longing, and
that memory is now a torment. The attempt to 'remember' it

fully and to understand herself fully in its context, serves
only to intensify dividedness into self-hatred:

> Viens, que je reconnaisse et que je les haïsse,
> Cette ombrageuse enfant, ce silence complice,
> Ce trouble transparent qui baigne dans les bois...
> (197)

The tender nostalgia which closes the eighth section is
insistently interrupted by the opening of the ninth:

> 'Que dans le ciel placés, mes yeux tracent mon
> temple!
> Et que sur moi repose un autel sans exemple!'
> Criaient de tout mon corps la pierre et la
> pâleur... (209)

The Fate's dividedness is complete. She can no longer
master her memories of temptation - that is, her 'secrète
soeur' - but can only look to release from her bondage to
sensibility in a self-sacrificing death. The earth, no
longer anything but a 'bandeau de couleur', she will
willingly leave and her body, 'cette rose sans prix', is
vowed to death. 'Je nous détruis ensemble', in the phrase
from the *Cahiers*.

At this moment, however, death gains an opponent for
the mind and body of the Fate - the spring which begins to
move in her veins. And it is in her veins that it moves;
insofar as the 'present' at least has a recognizable linear
form, it is clear that it is still night at this point, and
it is therefore from within that the Fate hears this appeal
to life and vigour. But if it comes from within, it nevertheless comes in the form of an *attack*, and the imagery is
brutal as well as lyrical:

> L'étonnant printemps rit, viole... On ne sait d'où
> Venu? (227)

123

The dialectic of the earlier part of the poem is reversed;
as with Teste's physical suffering, the effort to master and
control sensibility only makes its attack more 'external',
more of a violation, and more powerful:

> Quelle résisterait, mortelle, à ces remous?
> Quelle mortelle?
> Moi si pure, mes genoux
> Pressent les terreurs de genoux sans défense...
> L'air me brise. L'oiseau perce de cris d'enfance
> Inouïs... (243)

Against the appeal of spring and its conspiracy to enchain
her as mother in the eternal cycle of birth and death, the
Fate returns a refusal, opposing to biological continuity
the purity of her own consciousness, rejecting the spectres
who press in on her, demanding the life she can give:

> Je n'accorderai pas la lumière à des ombres,
> Je garde loin de vous l'esprit sinistre et
> clair... (274)

But even in this refusal there is an unobtrusive victory for
life:

> Et puis... mon coeur aussi vous refuse sa foudre.
> J'ai pitié de nous tous, ô tourbillons de poudre!
> (277)

By admitting 'mon coeur' next to 'l'esprit sinistre et
clair', by including herself among the 'tourbillons de
poudre' of humanity, the Fate has lost her battle and paved
the way for a more subtle attack. Her tear, imminent from
the opening of the poem, and long held back, begins to flow.

Like the vision of spring, the tear seems an external
agency, though it comes from sources deep within; it is
associated with the instincts she has just repudiated:

124

> D'où nais-tu?   Quel travail toujours triste et
> > nouveau
> Te tire avec retard, larme, de l'ombre amère?
> Tu gravis mes degrés de mortelle et de mère...
> > (292)

The Fate is no longer in control of herself; her body moves
without her volition, but with a mysterious confidence:

> Où va-t-il, sans répondre à sa propre ignorance,
> Ce corps dans la nuit noire étonné de sa foi?
> > (302)

She does not share that confidence; with an ironic memory of
the 'dureté précieuse' on which she used to rely, she calls
upon the earth to support her, but it is a 'terre trouble',
and the precipice awaits. In her confusion she calls
alternately on the swan-god of her temptation, the
treacherous earth, and her own body. Both death and total
surrender to the instincts of her body seem near.

The poem re-opens: 'Mystérieuse Moi, pourtant, tu vis
encore!' (325). As in the opening of the poem, the Fate
slowly becomes aware of herself and the world around, but
this time with sober acceptance of their distinctness one
from the other, and of the links which bind them:

> Regarde: un bras très pur est vu, qui se dénude.
> Je te revois, mon bras... Tu portes l'aube...
> > (333)

But the dawn is false, the awakening premature; and the
chain of reconciliations which constitutes the second part
of the poem is only slowly unwound. In one sense, those
reconciliations are dependent on the fact that no resolution
was reached in the night, no threshold crossed; the Fate
finds herself still enchained in her memories and desires,
and it is through the recapitulation of the 'events' of the

night that reconciliation is effected. Regretting that she
is still a 'victime inachevée', she taxes herself with folly
for not having obeyed the 'lucide dédain' which tempted her
to death. But a new dialectic now enters the picture;
instead of turning on her instincts and sensibility the
light of lucid self-consciousness, she turns it on that
other part of herself which had opposed instinct:

> Attente vaine, et vaine... Elle ne peut mourir
> Qui devant son miroir, pleure pour s'attendrir.
>
> (379)

Instead of seeing itself as *observer*, 'l'extrême attentive'
is grasped as having been itself a dramatic role, no more
fundamental to the self than the 'secrète soeur'. And with
that realization comes the problem of accounting for her
survival, for the continuity of the self- - 'Mystérieuse
Moi' - through its metamorphoses. The answer to the problem
is simple, even disarming:

> Le sais-je, quel reflux traître m'a retirée
> De mon extrémité pure et prématurée,
> Et m'a repris le sens de mon vaste soupir?
> Comme l'oiseau se pose, il fallut s'assoupir.
>
> (441)

The simple necessity of sleep preserved the continuity of
life, despite the dramas of the mind. Faced with this
realization, the Fate abdicates its transcendent preten-
sions, and accepts the condition of mortality with its
weakness which had proved a strength:

> Doucement,
> Me voici: mon front touche à ce consentement...
> Ce corps, je lui pardonne, et je goûte à la
> cendre. (451)

The sixteenth and final section, following the real

126

dawn and the Fate's definitive awakening, is composed of two subtly-rising cadences of reconciliation. In the first part, she addresses the 'couche' where she lay, recognizing its shape as hers. Reconciliation with her own body and the world outside with which the body is mysteriously linked are intertwined in the lines:

> Et ce jeune soleil de mes étonnements
> Me paraît d'une aïeule éclairer les tourments,
> Tant sa flamme aux remords ravit leur existence,
> Et compose d'aurore une chère substance
> Qui se formait déjà substance d'un tombeau!...
> O, sur toute la mer, sur mes pieds, qu'il est
>   beau! (487)

But the poem does not end with a closing of the cycle; the events of the night are not simply forgotten. To her question

> ... Alors, n'ai-je formé, vains adieux si je vis,
> Que songes? ... (495)

the Fate replies with a statement which, for all its lyrical fervour, is studded with hesitations and conditions. A simple return to Eden, if it ever existed, is not possible; but equally, there is no return to the proud temptations of the night, nor a simple surrender to vital instinct. The imagery of the Fate's final invocation to the sun is full of tension as well as reconciliation. Her stance -'l'être contre le vent' - is symbolic of a new relationship with the world. No longer 'l'épouse et l'égale du jour', she nonetheless consents to its radiance. She can no longer see herself as undivided, but she accepts her division, and refuses deliberate and self-conscious alienation. In this 'âpre éveil', self, body and world are seen as separate but irremediably enchained to one another, and capable of existing in a life-giving rather than a destructive tension:

127

>...Si je viens, en vêtements ravis,
> Sur ce bord, sans horreur, humer la haute écume,
> Boire des yeux l'immense et riante amertume,
> L'être contre le vent, dans le plus vif de l'air,
> Recevant au visage un appel de la mer...
> Alors, malgré moi-même, il le faut, ô Soleil,
> Que j'adore mon coeur où tu te viens connaître,
> Doux et puissant retour du délice de naître,
>
> Feu vers qui se soulève une vierge de sang
> Sous les espèces d'or d'un sein reconnaissant!
>
> (496)

If Mme. Goll's testimony is not to be entirely discounted, and if Rilke did indeed read *La Jeune Parque* in 1918, a very specific meaning can be attached to his sense of 'étrange parenté', his characterization of Valéry, as 'un autre moi-même'. Like the young Fate at the conclusion of the first half of the poem, Rilke had fallen silent with the tensions of his early work unresolved, his most recent work bearing witness to a sense of a self divided and inflexibly separated from the natural world, then to 'awake' after the war with an inexplicable sense of *continuity*. Read as a structure of reconciliations, the second part of *La Jeune Parque* must have echoed with an almost uncanny accuracy - even conceivably have encouraged and strengthened - the general mood of his first post-war verses:

> Letztes ist nicht, daß man sich überwinde...
>
> (II,242)

> Gekonnt hats keiner; denn das Leben währt
> weils keiner konnte...
> Weils keiner meistert, bleibt das Leben rein.
>
> (II,126)

The section of the poem which Mme. Goll recalls Rilke as reciting with particular emotion - the invocation to the tear - is entirely in keeping with such a possibility. If, however, a reading of *La Jeune Parque* in 1918 must remain surrounded by some uncertainty, it is certain that Rilke

read the three Odes - 'Aurore', 'Palme' and 'La Pythie' -
published together in 1920. Whilst his response to the
conclusion of 'Palme' - the commendation of patient
maturation - has been frequently noted, it has not been
generally appreciated that this specific 'lesson' forms part
of a general pattern of reconciliation apparent in the
three poems taken together.

Of all the poems published later as *Charmes*, 'La
Pythie' is closest to *La Jeune Parque*, even down to details
of imagery and vocabulary. Like the young Fate, Valéry's
Pythia is 'profondément mordue'. Like her, she regrets her
former state of harmony:

> Mon cher corps... Forme préférée,
> Fraîcheur par qui ne fut jamais
> Aphrodite désaltérée,
> Intacte nuit, tendres sommets,
> Et vos partages indicibles
> D'une argile en îles sensibles,
> Douce matière de mon sort,
> Quelle alliance nous vécûmes... (I,132)

Like her, she rebels against the 'invasion' which is both
awareness of physicality and self-consciousness:

> Pourquoi, Puissance Créatrice,
> Auteur du mystère animal,
> Dans cette vierge pour matrice,
> Semer les merveilles du mal!

Like her, she suffers a rising tide from within:

> Entends, mon âme, entends ces fleuves!
> Quelles cavernes sont ici?
> Est-ce mon sang?...

And, as from the young Fate, 'une voix nouvelle' of
reconciliation breaks as the final outcome. The resemblance
is not of course exact; Valéry's choice of protagonist and
his overt concern with poetic creation in this poem impose a

129

number of different emphases, but the general *curve* is
similar. As for 'Aurore' and 'Palme', we know that they
originally formed a single poem, divided - and later placed
as opening and conclusion to *Charmes* - in respect of their
complementary tonalities, one instinct with the vigour of
morning, the other celebrating patience and calm. Whether
in the major or the minor key, however, both poems sing of
balance, particularly of balance between the various aspects
of the self. In 'Aurore', the poet seeks 'dans ma forêt
sensuelle/Les oracles de mon chant', and exclaims:

> Voici mes vignes ombreuses,
> Les berceaux de mes hasards!
> Les images sont nombreuses
> A l'égal de mes regards... (I,112)

In 'Palme', the tree symbolizes the self in its hierarchical
structure, and celebrates the perfect inter-relationships of
height and depth:

> Admire comme elle vibre,
> Et comme une lente fibre
> Qui divise le moment,
> Départage sans mystère
> L'attirance de la terre
> Et le poids du firmament!
>
> Ce bel arbitre mobile
> Entre l'ombre et le soleil... (I,154)

In *La Jeune Parque*, on the hypothesis of a reading in 1918,
and without doubt in the three *Odes*, Rilke found a *general*
lesson of balance and reconciliation with respect to the
relationships of the self with itself, and with the world
around. As Valéry put it - prematurely - in the *Soirée
avec M. Teste*, 'je me suis détesté, je me suis adoré -
puis, nous avons vieilli ensemble' (II,15).

As we have seen, however, such moderate conclusions were not finally sufficient for Rilke, and if the hypothesis is to be sustained that the work of Valéry was of capital importance for him in the creative burst of 1922, it is to other works that we must turn - particularly to those two works for which he professed greatest admiration, 'Le Cimetière Marin' (translated immediately on discovery) and *L'Ame et la danse* (copied out in full on the eve of his final triumph). By way of introduction to these texts, however, it will be useful to discuss briefly the *Note et digression* added in 1919 to the early *Introduction à la méthode de Léonard de Vinci*.

The extent to which the narrative sequence of *La Jeune Parque* operates as a self-consciously deceptive device, a fiction within a fiction, has already been intimated. Valéry himself described his work as a circle - which he would have closed had it been possible. As for the conclusion, which seems to break out of the circle, it is noticeable that not all critics have found it entirely satisfactory, Hartman going so far as to call it 'an ambiguous and forced gesture', but without analysing in detail the circular features of the text which make it appear so.[94] That task has been undertaken more recently by Jean Levaillant,[95] in an analysis of the devices by which apparently functional oppositions within the text mirror each other, so undermining their conclusiveness, and of the various means - projection of dramatic selves, presentation of 'intervals' as 'transitions' - by which the young Fate creates the appearance of linear narrative and of spatialized order within the self out of an essentially circular trajectory around a central *void*. That void is the self, grasped in its immediacy, and the question which opens the poem - in effect, the one word 'Qui?' - is never answered,

131

only endlessly repeated; the entire discourse which the text
creates is an impossible attempt to fill this void created
by the inevitable *posteriority* of language to experience.
The self can only be grasped indirectly by a series of
mirrors, always retrospective; and in the conclusion, as
Levaillant observes, the roles of mirror and observer are
merely reversed, as the Fate calls upon the sun to 'know
itself' in her.[96]

The impossible question to which, in this analysis, the
young Fate addresses herself, is discussed more explicitly
in the *Note et digression*. Valéry's starting-point for this
crucial section of the text is Leonardo's - and the Church's
- 'materialism' which, in insisting on the necessity of a
body for the soul to inhabit, reduces the soul, in Valéry's
interpretation, to a 'minimum logique' (I,1214). Applying
this perspective to his own earlier observations in the
Introduction, he analyses with great finesse what he now
characterizes as the 'tentation de l'esprit'. Certain
passages of the text recall its predecessor directly, but
with a warier realization of the consequences of a certain
line of thinking. The (at least implied) dialectic of the
Introduction gives way to a *circular* movement. Where the
earlier text had noted that, faced with the 'world', 'nous
ne savons faire autre chose que nous en distinguer, pour
aussitôt nous y remettre' (I,1163f.), the mature Valéry
observes that the movement of withdrawal is so absorbing
that it precludes any return:

> Pour un présence d'esprit aussi sensible à elle-même,
> et qui se ferme sur elle-même par le détour de
> 'l'Univers', tous les événements de tous les genres,
> et la mort, et les pensées, ne lui sont que des *figures*
> subordonnées. Comme chaque *chose visible* est à la fois
> étrangère, indispensable, et inférieure à la *chose qui y*
> *voit*, ainsi l'importance de ces figures, si grande
> qu'elle apparaisse à chaque instant, pâlit à la réflex-
> ion devant la seule persistance de l'attention elle-même.
> (I,1217f.)

This transition from dialectic to circular movement is of course already given in the reflexiveness of the *Soirée avec M. Teste*. But the slightly quizzical note of the *Soirée* gives way in the *Note* to a more sombre tone as Valéry pushes his analysis to conclusions. If consciousness is to be 'isolated' from any possible object of consciousness, if in the 'palais fermé de miroirs' one seeks the 'lampe solitaire qu'ils enfantent à l'infini' (I,1216), it can only be as 'fille directe et ressemblante de l'être sans visage':

> Encore un peu, et elle ne compterait plus comme existences nécessaires que deux entités essentiellement inconnues: Soi et X. Toutes deux abstraites de tout, impliquées dans tout, impliquant tout. Égales et consubstantielles. (I,1222f.)

The theatre image in which Valéry imagines consciousness as a 'présence qui ne peut pas se contempler, condamnée au spectacle adverse' (I,1224), recalls the *Soirée*, but at this ultimate limit, Teste himself is reduced to actor rather than spectator. A few pages later, the entire drama of *La Jeune Parque* is effectively dismissed as a play of mere 'personality':

> ...elle n'est pas sûre d'être positivement *quelqu'un*; elle se déguise et se nie plus facilement qu'elle ne s'affirme. Tirant de sa propre inconsistance quelques ressources et beaucoup de vanité, elle met dans les fictions son activité favorite. Elle vit de romans, elle épouse sérieusement mille personnages. Son héros n'est jamais soi-même... (I,1227)

There is no possible incarnation for the 'moi pur'; it exists only as 'élément unique et monotone de l'être même dans le monde', as 'cette profonde *note* de l'existence' (I,1228), or, more abstractly, as an 'invariant', devoid of content (I,1230).

Valéry's text is perhaps the most philosophically

satisfying of this anti-philosophical thinker. But the
existential basis of his thought is not to be ignored. The
attempt to see consciousness as a form of transcendence,
epiphenomenal but incarnate, corresponds to a certain form
of anxiety:

> C'est une manière de lumineux supplice que de sentir
> que l'on voit tout, sans cesser de sentir que l'on
> est encore *visible*, et l'objet concevable d'une
> attention étrangère; et sans se trouver jamais le poste
> ni le regard qui ne laissent rien derrière eux.
>
> (I,1217)

The displacements of the early texts, reducing the world to
pure visibility and defining the poetic self as 'la chose
qui y voit', are described exactly in the *Note* in the
following terms:

> Tous les phénomènes, par là frappés d'une sorte d'égale
> répulsion, et comme rejetés successivement par un geste
> identique, apparaissent dans une certaine équivalence
> ... Il faut bien comprendre que rien n'échappe à la
> rigueur de cette exhaustion; mais qu'il suffit de notre
> attention pour mettre les mouvements les plus intimes
> au rang des événements et des objets extérieurs.
>
> (I,1225)

Given the form of Valéry's analysis, the consequences are
inescapable. But as existential wager, embraced eagerly in
the *Introduction*, they are described now as 'cette solitude
... cette netteté désespérée', preparing the way for a
certain form of 'ennui':

> Couleur et douleur; souvenirs, attente et surprises;
> cet arbre, et le flottement de son feuillage, et sa
> variation annuelle et son ombre comme sa substance,
> ses accidents de figure et de position, les pensées
> très éloignées qu'il rappelle à ma distraction, -

in other words, all that the early text had celebrated as
the delight of 'l'homme de l'esprit' -

tout cela est égal... Toutes choses se substituent,
- ne serait-ce pas la définition des *choses*? (I,1225)

'*Durus est hic sermo*', comments Valéry wryly at one
point. Without doubt, Rilke found it so; *Note et digression*
was one of those texts of Valéry which he admired at some
distance, and it has been discussed here principally as a
necessary transition from the 'surface' structure of *La
Jeune Parque* to the fundamental structure of 'Le Cimetière
Marin', most personal and existentially direct of Valéry's
works.

    *   *   *   *   *   *   *   *

La plupart des gens y voient par l'intellect bien plus
souvent que par les yeux...Sachant horizontal le
niveau des eaux tranquilles, ils méconnaissent que la
mer est *debout* au fond de la vue. (I,1165,6)

Valéry's early observation from the *Introduction* is echoed
across the years in the opening of the 'Cimetière marin':

Ce toit tranquille, où marchent des colombes,
Entre les pins palpite, entre les tombes...
                                        (I,147)

The *substitution* of roof for sea, and of doves for sails,
echoes the 'rejection' of the analytic mind of mere
'choses'. As in the early poems too, this displacement is
accompanied by a vision of the world as engaged in a system
of transformations, here a transformation of endless
flickering motion into immobility:

Midi le juste y compose de feux
La mer, la mer toujours recommencée!...
Quel pur travail de fins éclairs consume
Maint diamant d'imperceptible écume,
Et quelle paix semble se concevoir!

But this transformation is not purely an object of observation; the whole scene is consubstantial with the self:

> O mon silence!... Édifice dans l'âme,
> Mais comble d'or aux mille tuiles, Toit!

The 'scintillation sereine', the 'dédain souverain' of sea and sun is offered to the gods as the *poet's* 'offrande suprême'. Where the heroine of *La Jeune Parque* slowly dissociates herself from the chaotic world into which she wakes, the poet of 'Le Cimetière marin' rapidly integrates himself into a world of ordered calm, 'closing on himself' 'par le détour de l'Univers'. Whereas *La Jeune Parque* projects linear narrative, this poem projects a spatialized hierarchy, figuring a certain series of relationships within the self, and within that hierarchy, 'la substance chatoyante et mobile de notre durée' (I,1211) is transformed into pure radiance, a paradoxical 'Temple du Temps'. The metamorphosis moves towards absence, pure negation, in the image of the transposition of fruit into immaterial delight, of shore into pure audibility, and of the self into 'future fumée'.

J.R. Lawler has commented on the play of images of *looking* in the opening stanzas:

> Le protagoniste a contemplé la scène ('un long regard'), trouvé que la mer le regardait ('Oeil'), s'est identifié à la mer ('mon regard marin'), a demandé au ciel de le regarder ('regarde-moi') et finalement demandé au ciel de se regarder en lui ('regarde-toi').[97]

Like the young Fate, the protagonist of the 'Cimetière marin' turns to the sun, figuring here the confrontation of 'Soi et X' of the *Note*, 'égales et consubstantielles'. But that confrontation is always hypothetical, always 'encore un peu' further on, unimaginable save in an impossible disincarnation. The conclusion of this series of 'regards' - 'Mais rendre la lumière / Suppose d'ombre une morne moitié' - is thus not a mere sophistry; it represents the 'lumineux supplice' of visibility, of continued incarnation. And as in the *Note*, there is no escape from - or definitively *into* - that incarnation; in turning from scene as self to self as content, the protagonist discovers only the 'creux toujours futur'.

The intimations of mortality arising from the graveyard are at first complaisantly recuperated in celebration of that void, that *absence*: 'La vie est vaste, étant ivre d'absence'. But Leonardo's 'materialism', his definition of death as 'désastre *pour l'âme*', dissolves that complaisance. In the central thirteenth stanza, the elements of the poem's metaphorical structure are juxtaposed in a different configuration from that which governs the opening:

> Les morts cachés sont bien dans cette terre
> Qui les réchauffe et sèche leur mystère.
> Midi là-haut, Midi sans mouvement
> En soi se pense et convient à soi-même...
> Tête complète et parfait diadème,
> Je suis en toi le secret changement.

'Midi' is still the image of a self-sufficient, self-regarding consciousness, but it is not the living poet whose condition is figured thereby; only the dead approach that degree of purity:

> Tu n'as que moi pour contenir tes craintes!
> Mes repentirs, mes doutes, mes contraintes
> Sont le défaut de ton grand diamant...
> Mais dans leur nuit toute lourde de marbres,
> Un peuple vague aux racines des arbres
> A pris déjà ton parti lentement.

137

The earlier postulation of a metamorphosis towards immaterial radiance is echoed ironically in the characterization of the dead as 'fondu dans une absence épaisse'.

The circle tightens rather than loosens its grip, however, by this impatient dismissal of death as 'consolatrice'. For it is towards disincarnation that consciousness necessarily aspires, and consciousness, though opposed to life, is yet a function *of* life. The innermost recesses of the self can neither be named nor externalized as object of intentional direction:

> Le vrai rongeur, le ver irréfutable
> N'est point pour vous qui dormez sous la table,
> Il vit de vie, il ne me quitte pas!
>
> Amour, peut-être, ou de moi-même haine?
> Sa dent secrète est de moi si prochaine
> Que tous les noms lui peuvent convenir!

Thought itself cannot but spatialize our 'durée', as Zeno's paradoxes imprison movement in spatial relationships:

> Zénon! Cruel Zénon! Zénon d'Élée!
> M'as-tu percé de cette flèche ailée
> Qui vibre, vole et qui ne vole pas!

Mobility appears as impossible as immobility - except by the passing of that spark across the impossible gap into 'l'ère successive', not recuperated, as in *La Jeune Parque*, into transition, but grasped *as* interval, as intermittence between consciousness and life. 'Brisez, mon corps, cette forme pensive!'

But the conclusion of the poem is not simply an upsurge of vital energy. In the final stanzas it moves toward a further re-assemblage of its component metaphors. The poet

cannot escape the metamorphosis of stanzas five and fifteen;
but it proceeds, not towards radiance, nor (so long as life
continues) towards clay. The opening designation of the sea
as 'toujours recommencée' is re-interpreted to allow a
further and this time definitive identification of poet and
scene. For the metamorphosis of the sea, 'fausse captive'
of the only apparently eternal moment of 'Midi', is only
apparently towards radiance. In being freed from the
immobility of noon, returned to its condition of 'puissance
salée', the sea offers a powerful image of an *inclusive*
circle which is the only escape from the *exclusive* circle of
Zeno's paradoxes, the authentic circle as opposed to the
inauthentic 'parfait diadème' of the sun; For the sea is

> Hydre absolue, ivre de ta chair bleue,
> Qui te remords l'étincelante queue
> Dans un tumulte au silence pareil...

Each item of that description echoes an element of the opening: 'ivre de ta chair bleue' contrasts with 'ivre
d'absence'; 'un tumulte au silence pareil' with 'quelle
paix'. But the contrasts are not ironic. The endless
tumult of the sea *is* like silence, the hydra *is* absolute.
The motion of the sea resolves itself into the image of the
serpent biting its own tail. It is *beyond* change, not in
escape from change, that a constant lies - the very consistency of change itself. The incarnation of the disincarnate
void of the 'moi pur' is in the perpetual metamorphoses of
the self around this invariant, no longer a citadel to be
defended, but the 'still point of the turning world' of the
self, itself a system of dynamic exchange.

*   *   *   *   *   *   *   *

L'*Ame et la danse* is no doubt one of the more dated of
Valéry's major works; the shades of Socrates, Phaedrus and
Eryximachus are accompanied a little too evidently by those

of Loie Fuller and Njinsky, and much of the particularities
of the dialogue is dictated by Valéry's animus against
systematizing philosophy. But into its sinuous and multi-
layered development are woven themes which tease out into
linear progression the densely-packed imagery of the final
stanzas of the 'Cimetière marin'. To avoid premature
conclusions, however, it will be as well to sketch a *general*
account of the text in the context of Valéry's previously
examined works, leaving until later consideration of Rilke's
no doubt partial reading.

The dialogue opens on a semi-humorous note of lassitude
and discouragement. Sated with food and drink, Eryximachus
turns for intellectual nourishment to Socrates, who is
occupied with observing the scene before him. 'L'homme qui
mange', he remarks, 'est le plus juste des hommes' (II,149)

'Voici déjà l'énigme', returns the doctor, and indeed
Socrates's observation leads directly into the opening
themes of the work with a movement from the physiological to
the psychological which is to be characteristic. As each
mouthful that a man takes nourishes indifferently his
virtues and his vices, so the mind feeds indifferently on
truth and error, reality and dream.

> C'est la vie même qui le veut: tu le sais mieux que
> moi, qu'elle se sert de tout. Tout lui est bon,
> Eryximaque, pour ne jamais conclure. C'est là ne
> conclure qu'à elle-même... N'est-elle pas ce mouvement
> mystérieux qui, par le détour de tout ce qui arrive,
> me transforme incessamment en moi-même, et qui me
> ramène assez promptement à ce même Socrate pour que je
> le retrouve, et que m'imaginant nécessairement de le
> reconnaître, *je sois*! (II,151)

Passing from the physiological through the philosophical -
or rather, the anti-philosophical - Socrates arrives at the
existential; the continuity of the self is grasped only

a posteriori, and perhaps as an illusion. There is a
certain lassitude in Socrates's words which prepare the
way for his later diagnosis of life as 'ennui', but the
image with which he pursues his thoughts - the seminal
image of the whole dialogue - at the same time points a
way beyond that 'ennui'. Life is

> une femme qui danse, et qui cesserait divinement
> d'être femme, si le bond qu'elle a fait, elle y
> pouvait obéir jusqu'aux nues. (II,151)

Immediately, however, the image is a signal for the entrance
of the actual dancers. Socrates's train of thought is only
momentarily interrupted. Phaedrus begins to dream
voluptuously, and is tartly reminded that what he witnesses
is the opposite of dream, an order from which chance has
been abolished. And yet, 'le contraire d'un rêve, qu'est-
ce, Phèdre, sinon quelque autre rêve?' If life is a
dancer, 'la pensée des Immortels' which governs life is
figured in 'ces nobles similitudes, les conversions, les
inversions, les diversions inépuisables qui se répondent et
se déduisent sous nos yeux' (II,155), and the observer's
apprehension of those endless transformations constitutes
'les connaissances divines'.

The first part of the dialogue is brought toward a
conclusion by the entrance of the principal *danseuse*, 'la
divine Athikté', whose first figures bring the dialogue to
the point of resolution, or *almost* so; After a 'walk'
which Eryximachus describes as 'le suprême de son art'
(II,156), she stops, and her cessation itself seems
momentous:

> Instant absolument vierge. Et puis, instant où
> quelque chose doit se rompre dans l'âme, dans
> l'attente, dans l'assemblée... Quelque chose se

rompre... Et cependant c'est aussi comme une
soudure. (II,158)

As she moves again, it is with a leap which brings to life
Socrates's image, and almost promises to accomplish that
'bond...jusqu'aux nues' which would transport her into a
higher condition:

> Oh! la voici enfin, qui entre dans l'exception et qui
> pénètre dans ce qui n'est pas possible... (II,159)

But as Socrates had observed, such a leap is always
impossible, and the dancer 'becomes herself' again, reducing
the dialogue itself to a lower level of tension.

The conversation proceeds with attempts to define the
art of dance. Phaedrus's naive enjoyment is contrasted with
Socrates's urge to penetrate to the heart of the matter, but
it is Phaedrus who sets in motion the play of definitions,
with a characterization of dance as 'l'âme des fables'
(II,162). Socrates demurs, and pressed by his companion to
admit that the dance represents *something*, replies:

> Nulle chose, cher Phèdre. Mais toute chose,
> Eryximaque. Aussi bien l'amour comme la mer, et la vie
> elle-même, et les pensées... Ne sentez-vous pas
> qu'elle est l'acte pur des métamorphoses? (II,164f.)

'Toutes choses se substituent', Valéry had written in the
Note et digression; 'ne serait-ce pas la définition des
choses?' Dance, as an act of metamorphosis which is *pure*,
shorn of all directly representational value, symbolizes the
accidents of life reduced to their *figures*.

The status of the participants in this dialogue as
observers recalls the theatre image of that same *Note*, and
further back, the theatre scene of the *Soirée avec M. Teste*,

142

whose shade hovers over the dialogue briefly as Eryximachus
and then Socrates conjure up in opposition to Phaedrus's
rhapsodies that 'oeil froid' which sees in the dance only
unreason and madness:

> Il suffit que l'âme se fixe et se refuse, pour ne plus
> concevoir que l'étrangeté et le dégoût de cette
> agitation ridicule... Que si tu veux, mon âme, tout
> ceci est absurde! (II,163)

The delight of Valéry's early Leonardo in that power of
analysis which, from a detached point of observation,
reduces the transformations of reality to a series of
figures, appears in the first part of *L'Ame et la danse* in
the spectators' delight in the 'foison multicolore' before
them. But the dialogue does not end there; Socrates's
confession of confusion following on from his own apparently
conclusive definition of dance as 'l'acte pur des
métamorphoses' signifies that it is capable of other
interpretations from that which the first part of the
dialogue implies. The transition to the second half is
marked first by Socrates's rejection of the stasis implied
in his detachment - 'mon désir est mouvement, Eryximaque'
(II,165) - and then by an apparent turn to a quite unrelated,
though not unprepared, theme, that of 'ennui':

> J'entends, sache-le bien, non l'ennui passager; non
> l'ennui par fatigue, ou l'ennui dont on voit le germe,
> ou celui dont on sait les bornes; mais cet ennui
> parfait, ce pur ennui...cet ennui enfin, qui n'a
> d'autre substance que la vie même, et d'autre cause
> seconde que la clairvoyance du vivant. Cet ennui
> absolu n'est en soi que la vie toute nue, quand elle
> se regarde clairement. (II,167)

The theme is drawn back into relationship with other
themes in the dialogue - firstly, with that of the nature of
truth launched in the opening speeches of the dialogue.

In Eryximachus's diagnosis, 'connaissance' is that excess, that superfluity over pure being, which is introduced by the human mind, and which is the source of all error and duplicity, the 'mille masques' which cover life, and protect us from 'le réel, à l'état pur' and inevitable 'ennui' (II,168). Secondly, the theme of 'ennui' is related to the major theme of the dialogue by the remedy Socrates proposes:

> Tu ne vois donc pas, Eryximaque, que parmi toutes les ivresses, la plus noble, et la plus ennemie du grand ennui, est l'ivresse due à nos actes? Nos actes, et singulièrement ceux de nos actes qui mettent notre corps en branle, peuvent nous faire entrer dans un état étrange et admirable... C'est l'état le plus éloigné de ce triste état où nous avons laissé l'observateur lucide et immobile que nous imaginâmes tout à l'heure. (II,169)

Against this 'observateur lucide et immobile' Socrates conjures up a comparison of Athikté to the salamander which lives and prospers in fire, inside the very flame, just as the dancer seems to inhabit 'une essence très subtile de musique et de mouvement' (II,170).

At this moment Athikté's dance begins a *presto* movement which seems to hurry Socrates and the dialogue towards their conclusions. Socrates's long speech which follows abandons the questing, analytic formulations of the earlier part of the dialogue in favour of exclamations and aphorisms, as attempts to define the condition of flame in terms of the dance taking place before his eyes. Flame is defined generally as 'chose vive et divine' (II,171), and more specifically in two ways which each answer to the main themes of the dialogue. First, flame is 'le moment même':

> Ce qu'il y a de fol, et de joyeux, et de formidable dans l'instant même!... Flamme est l'acte de ce moment qui est entre la terre et le ciel. O mes amis, tout ce qui passe de l'état lourd à l'état subtil, passe par le moment de feu et de lumière...

'Ce qu'il y a de fol, et de joyeux' answers to Socrates's ennui', but the moment is not only one of joy, but also of transition to some other condition.

Secondly, flame is 'la forme insaisissable et fière de la plus noble destruction':

> ...la grande Danse, ô mes amis, n'est-elle point cette délivrance de notre corps tout entier possédé par l'esprit du mensonge, et de la musique qui est mensonge, et ivre de la négation de la nulle réalité?

Some 'excess' over the nullity of reality is required by the human condition, and is provided by the dynamic exchanges figured in dance and flame:

> Ce corps s'exerce dans toutes ses parties, et se combine à lui-même, et se donne forme après forme, et il sort incessamment de soi! Le voici enfin dans cet état comparable à la flamme, au milieu des échanges les plus actifs... (II,172)

A propos of *Eupalinos*, Valéry commented, in a letter to Paul Souday, that he did not dismiss philosophy as such, only philosophers who imagined that they could seek 'truth' rather than 'la découverte ou la construction de quelque *forme*' (II,1400). In *L'Ame et la danse*, a number of *boutades* betray Valéry's scepticism concerning the possibility of metaphysical verities, but the comparison between mind and dancing body which Socrates draws here points to Valéry's evaluation of 'acts' of the mind and of the creative imagination as remedies for the complementary negativities of 'Soi et X', pure 'being' and pure reflexive consciousness:

> Cet *Un* veut jouer à *Tout*. Il veut jouer à l'universalité de l'âme! Il veut remédier à son identité par le nombre de ses actes! (II,171f.)

145

Exclusive, self-reflexive circularity as a means to
'universality' gives way to abundance; Teste's refusal of
the 'impurity' of production is itself refused in favour of
the pursuit of form, no single one of which exhausts, however, the power to create form.

The dialogue is not yet over, however. At the outset,
Socrates had passed from the philosophical to the
existential in a critique of the structure of the self, and
his primary theme is that of *life*. In the closing pages,
the *a posteriori* nature of all discourse with respect to
experience is symbolized by a reversal of roles between
observer and observed. On the occasion of the first appearance of the troupe, Socrates's own words had seemed to
summon up the dancers - 'A peine tu parles', Phaedrus had
observed, 'tu engendres ce qu'il faut' (II,151). Now it is
Athikté who dictates the pace of the dialogue. Socrates
returns to his first image of dance as an attempt at
transcendence, inevitably unsuccessful, merely 'fragments
d'un temps étranger, des bonds désespérés hors de sa forme
...' (II,172). But at this moment Athikté commences a final
supreme movement, and Socrates's conclusion is denied by
Phaedrus's breathless interruption:

> Regarde, mais regarde!... Elle danse là-bas et donne
> aux yeux ce qu'ici tu essayes de nous dire...Elle dérobe
> à la nature des attitudes impossibles, sous l'oeil
> même du Temps!... Il se laisse tromper... Elle
> traverse impunément l'absurde...

Socrates himself is convinced by *experience*:

> Moi-même, je me sens envahi de forces extraordinaires...
> Ou je sens qu'elles sortent de moi qui ne savais pas que
> je contenais ces vertus...tout est possible d'une
> autre manière; tout peut recommencer indéfiniment...

The last phrase echoes 'la mer toujours recommencée' of the
'Cimetière marin', and it is a similar re-interpretation to
that of the poem which brings the dialgoue to its definitive

climax. For Athikté does *not* leap; she *turns*:

> Elle tourne sur elle-même...
> Elle tourne, et tout ce qui est visible, se détache
> de son âme...

'Tout ce qui est visible' - the attempt to escape from
'visibility' takes the form, in Valéry's early work, of a
series of displacements, a 'détachement sans repos' ending
in the 'netteté désespérée', the 'palais fermé de miroirs'
of the *Note*. No transcendence is possible through a 'leap'
into disincarnation; but in the never-definitive, ever-
changing incarnations of the *moment*, 'toute la vase de son
âme se sépare enfin du plus pur' (II,174). To use the
governing metaphor of *L'Ame et la danse*, stasis, continuity,
is only glimpsed through ceaseless movement. In the opening
of *Eupalinos* (one of the fragments read by Rilke in 1921),
Socrates and Phaedrus had contemplated the river of Time:

> Cette nappe immense et accidentée, qui se précipite
> sans répit, roule vers le néant toutes les couleurs.
> Vois comme elle est terne dans l'ensemble. (II,80)

Such a reduction of life's multiplicity to a dull uniformity
is a result of the speaker's standpoint, for he and his
interlocutor are shades in the underworld:

> C'est que tu assistes à l'écoulement vrai des êtres,
> toi immobile dans la mort.

The river mocks Socrates's life-time ambition - to achieve
a condition of abstracted and motionless calm from the flux
of life, the better to judge its phenomena. In death he
achieves that end, and sees its futility:

> Je plaçais la Sagesse dans la posture éternelle où nous
> sommes. Mais d'ici tout est méconnaissable. La vérité
> est devant nous, et nous ne comprenons plus rien.

That disillusion is carried through into the lassitude of
L'Ame et la danse, to be answered finally in the whirling
motion of Athikté, 'immobile au centre même de son mouvement' (II,174), and in her own, and almost only, words, the
final ones of the dialogue:

> Asile, asile, ô mon asile, ô Tourbillon! - J'étais
> en toi, ô mouvement, en dehors de toutes les choses...
> (II,176)

*   *   *   *   *   *   *   *

It would be misleading to suggest, if only by the
implications of silence, that *L'Ame et la danse* represents,
in Valéry's work as a whole, a definitive term to his
questioning of the nature of the self. In purely
chronological terms, Valéry's career was at its mid-point in
1921, and in any case, 'conclusiveness' of any kind was
anathema to him. The displacement represented by Edmond
Teste remained a powerful investigative tool for Valéry as
thinker, and the 'Cycle Teste' itself continued to grow by
the addition of further short texts until his death. But
what 'Le Cimetière marin' and *L'Ame et la danse* do
represent is a revision of the existential consequences -
the consequences, that is, for the *whole* self - of Valéry's
fundamental hypothesis, closely linked with the revision
that hypothesis itself undergoes between the *Introduction à
la méthode de Léonard de Vinci* and the *Note et digression*.
And at an existential level, it is the poetry which reflects
this revision most clearly, in its attempt to embody the
workings of the self as an entire structure, not limited to
the early identification of that structure with reflexive
consciousness. As Christine Crow puts it, poems, for
Valéry, represented 'an attempt to restore...the
irreducibility of individual experience', to 'combine the
insights of formalism with the quality of subjective
experience'.[98] Though nothing could be more different in

148

tone from the breathless conclusion of *L'Ame et la danse* than the measured cadences of 'Les Pas', the groundwork, the fundamental dialectic is similar. The self exists only in becoming, not in being; it is a rhythm of exchange whose dynamics are determined by experience. But part of that rhythm is the return to the centre of the web, the 'empty centre' around which the transformations take place, and preserve the fundamental *sense* of the self.

VII. TRANSFORMATION AND SUBSISTENCE

Die Sonette an Orpheus and later verse

In *Das Stundenbuch*, the silence which precedes the first
poem is broken by the striking of the hour, summoning the
world to the presence of the poet; in the *Duineser Elegien* by
the cry of the poet, summoning the Angels to bear witness of
the human condition; in the *Sonette an Orpheus* by the song of
the god, creating a new order of silence, and summoning the
poet to admiration. The first proposes a world open to
creative intervention; the second a world whose relatedness
both with itself and the poet is dimly and fragmentarily
perceived; the third a world of total relatedness before
which the poet stands.

The first two Sonnets, forming a continuous 'narration',
have roots deep in Rilke's earlier work. The motif of
summoning may be followed through from that first summoning
of *Das Stundenbuch* through 'Wendung' -

>   Tiere traten getrost
>   in den offenen Blick, weidende...

to the opening Sonnet:

>   Tiere aus Stille drangen aus dem klaren
>   gelösten Wald von Lager und Genist...

The contrast of silence and order with 'Brüllen, Schrei,
Geröhr', on the other hand, goes back to 'Die Rosenschale',
while the conclusion of that poem -

> ...die Welt da draußen
> und Wind und Regen und Geduld des Frühlings
> und Schuld und Unruh und vermummtes Schicksal
> und Dunkelheit der abendlichen Erde
> bis auf der Wolken Wandel, Flucht und Anflug,
> bis auf den vagen Einfluß ferner Sterne
> in eine Hand voll Innres zu verwandeln.

is echoed in the second Sonnet:

> ...Und alles war ihr Schlaf.
> Die Bäume, die ich je bewundert, diese
> fühlbare Ferne, die gefühlte Wiese
> und jedes Staunen, das mich selbst betraf.

> Sie schlief die Welt.

The re-emergence of these themes, however, covers a series of crucial changes. The summoning of *Das Stundenbuch* is taken up in 'Wendung' only to be renounced, and the transformation effected by the roses of 'Die Rosenschale' is thrown into question by 'Waldteich', companion-piece to 'Wendung'. As those two poems make clear, the summoning of the natural world into the inner space of the self is undermined by the lack of an inner space commensurate with 'die großgewohnten Dinge'. So that if these motifs of summoning and transformation recur, it is not likely that it will be without some change of perspective.

One such change is readily apparent. Whereas in *Das Stundenbuch* it is the poet who summons, the Orphic summoning and transformation takes place within a totally mythic space in which the poet is present only as rapt observer, or better, hearer:

> Da stieg ein Baum. O reine Übersteigung!
> O Orpheus singt! O hoher Baum im Ohr!

And the hearing itself is a product of the Orphic power:

> ...da schufst du ihnen Tempel im Gehör.

Indeed, the form of the opening lines suggests that there is

no real distinction between the singing and the hearing, the
silence and the song. There is simply an existence, a
situation, which may be described as silence or as song - or
as sleep, as the second Sonnet has it. And that sleep or
song enters into the poet:

Und schlief in mir. Und alles war ihr Schlaf.

As was observed, the tragic dynamic of the Elegies was
determined at the outset by the definition of the Angels as
what we are not. So also the dynamic of the Sonnets is
determined by the relationship between *their* presiding deity
and the poet who inhabits the world over which he presides.
And these relationships in turn define the relationship
between poet and the third protagonist of the Rilkean drama,
the natural world. Though the Elegies move rapidly from
Angel to man, and from man to beast and tree, the movements
are in the form of contrasts, and there is, despite the
Hulewicz-letter, no real converse. Though the song of
Orpheus, by creating the power of hearing as well as the
song which is heard, apparently creates a closed circle like
that of the angelic 'Rückkehr zu sich', beast and tree are
caught up in it and it flows, bearing them, through the poet.

The role of the poet in this symbolic representation of
a world of total relatedness might then appear to be purely
passive, simply by-passing the questioning, found in the
poems of the critical years, of the poet's active
participation 'an dem, was *ist*'. But that questioning is
itself far from absent from the Sonnets, and it is through
that questioning that the nature of the poet's participation
is suggested.

The implicit formula of the first two Sonnets is that
existence is song. Reversing that eminently reversible
formula, the third declares: 'Gesang ist Dasein', but
continues:

152

>   ...Für den Gott ein Leichtes.
> Wann aber *sind* wir? Und wann wendet *er*
> an unser Sein die Erde und die Sterne?

The juxtaposition of the two questions is a pregnant form of
the long-matured intuition that a state of existential
grace, a sense of relatedness with the natural world, and
the possibility of true song, are indivisible. And human
consciousness remains as problematical as ever:

>   Sein Sinn ist Zwiespalt. An der Kreuzung zweier
>   Herzwege steht kein Tempel für Apoll.

The same Sonnet limns in the nature of true song, and again
the antecedents are clear, from the 'dispossession' theme of
the years 1912 to 1915 to the opening of the seventh Elegy:

>   Gesang, wie du ihn lehrst, ist nicht Begehr,
>   nicht Werbung um ein endlich noch Erreichtes...

But where the seventh Elegy moves from renunciation of
'Werbung' to the conservative task of preserving the shapes
of human experience, the Sonnet defines song as
>   Ein Hauch um nichts. Ein Wehn im Gott. Ein Wind.
And *that* image is carried forward into the next Sonnet:

>   O ihr Zärtlichen tretet zuweilen
>   in den Atem, der euch nicht meint,
>   laßt ihn an euren Wangen sich teilen,
>   hinter euch zittert er, wieder vereint.

Existence is song, song is breath, wind, the medium in which
and by which we live; though it is not intended for us, we
may step into it.

But the question remains: how are we to step into that
breath in such a way that it *is* 'wieder vereint'? For the

Orphic circle is *there* - in the Russian horse, for example:

>Der sang und der hörte -, dein Sagenkreis
>war *in* ihm geschlossen. (SI,xx)

A fountain-basin is

>Ein Ohr der Erde. Nur mit sich allein
>redet sie also. (SII,xv)

But the horse's consciousness is not divided; and the
metaphor of the circle poses its own problems:

>...Schiebt ein Krug sich ein,
>so scheint es ihr, daß du sie unterbrichst.

How are we *not* to 'interrupt'?

Unlike the Elegies, the Sonnets are not 'argumentative'
in form; they take the shape rather of a series of inter-
locking images. And in pursuing the images of singing and
hearing, the first part of the cycle concludes with a use
of the image for the *human* condition:

>O du verlorener Gott! Du unendliche Spur!
>Nur weil dich reißend zuletzt die Feindschaft
>   verteilte,
>sind wir die Hörenden jetzt und ein Mund der
>   Natur. (SI,xxvi)

The 'Sagenkreis' can be closed through man, the Sonnets
claim - and this is made possible through Orpheus's death.
And so one is led back to the sequence which celebrates that
event. Only to find that there is to be no celebration in
the traditional sense:

>Errichtet keinen Denkstein. Laßt die Rose
>nur jedes Jahr zu seinen Gunsten blühn. (SI,v)

For - pursuing the chain of identifications which mark the

Sonnets - Orpheus is song:

> Denn Orpheus ists. Seine Metamorphose
> in dem und dem. Wir sollen uns nicht mühn
>
> um andre Namen. Ein für alle Male
> ists Orpheus, wenn es singt. Er kommt und geht.

'Er kommt und geht' - a formula which reverberates throughout the cycle - is both an indication of the transience of a
single life, and of the Rilkean version of the eternal
recurrence, and entrance to the latter is only by way of the
former.

Insofar as assent to transience is an assent to death,
the Sonnet seems one more variation on the most consistent
of all Rilkean themes. But the development of the theme
here is significantly different from its development in the
Elegies. The state of grace which is inseparable from true
song is achieved through assent *to* death, but not *through*
death; the song of Orpheus is the song of the living, and
the poet's ever-repeated span of life, however brief, is
precious:

> Ists nicht schon viel, wenn er die Rosenschale
> um ein paar Tage manchmal übersteht?

The Sonnets do not move into the landscape of the dead.
They fulfil, as the ninth and tenth Elegies do not, the
insight of the first:

> Die ewige Strömung
> reißt durch beide Bereiche alle Alter
> immer mit sich und übertönt sie in beiden. (EI,83)

> Ist er ein Hiesiger? Nein, aus beiden
> Reichen erwuchs seine weite Natur. (SI,vi)

155

The Greek myth itself, especially that part of it concerning Orpheus's visit to and return from the underworld, is in evidence in the background of Rilke's reworking and assists in the resolution of this most problematical of Rilke's metaphor/concepts:

> Kündiger böge die Zweige der Weiden
> wer die Wurzeln der Weiden erfuhr.

This Sonnet might be compared to the earlier use of the Orpheus/Eurydice myth in the *Neue Gedichte*. Eurydice, in the earlier version, *became* 'Wurzel'; in the Sonnet, the Orphic *experience* of 'Wurzeln' strengthens his song. There, Eurydice is an object of passive dissolution, and Orpheus is silent; here, *his* dissolution *is* song:

> ...während dein Klang noch in Löwen und Felsen
> verweilte,
> und in den Bäumen und Vögeln. Dort singst du
> noch jetzt. (SI,xxvi)

From the point of view of the theme of death, it is the *Sonette an Orpheus*, not the 1922 Elegies, which form the apposite resolution of the question of 1912:

> Ist die Sage umsonst, daß einst in der Klage um
> Linos
> wagende erste Musik dürre Erstarrung durchdrang;
> daß erst im erschrockenen Raum, dem ein beinah
> göttlicher Jüngling
> plötzlich für immer enttrat, das Leere in jene
> Schwingung geriet, die uns jetzt hinreißt und
> tröstet und hilft. (EI,91)

The necessary tonality of death enters into the Orphic song without overwhelming it; the Orphic assent to death is an aspect of assent to a totality of life-and-death which, in dwelling and grave, is the realm of his song:

Nichts kann das gültige Bild ihm verschlimmern;
sei es aus Gräbern, sei es aus Zimmern,
rühme er Fingerring, Spange und Krug. (SI,vi)

There are few, if any, new elements in the Sonnets
which make a significant contribution to the total
resolution which they offer; their achievement lies not in
new images, so much as in a symbolic framework which draws
together without strain the disparate concepts and images,
the exploration of which constitutes the major part of
Rilke's poetic career. If the Sonnets appear as the
appropriate resolution of the themes of the 1912 Elegies,
the reason for this is rather to be seen in the *dis-
appearance* of certain elements which in 1922 blocked any
satisfactory resolution. One such element is certainly the
intransigent insistence on a certain absoluteness of
conclusion which leads into the bleak and one-sided emphasis
of the tenth Elegy, a one-sidedness which is corrected in
the Sonnets. The other major blocking element is in
evidence in the ninth Elegy, and while the intransigent
absoluteness of the fourth, eighth and tenth Elegies may be
attributed to the depth and bitterness of Rilke's despair in
those years, this other element has roots far back in his
earliest work.

Eurydice was not *only* described as 'Wurzel':

Sie war in einem neuen Mädchentum
und unberührbar; ihr Geschlecht war zu
wie eine junge Blume gegen Abend...

Such was the first explicit appearance, in 1904, of an image
of self-containment that Rilke pursued unceasingly through
nearly twenty years. In the major poem, it is allied with
images of outward-streaming energy - perhaps a trifle
contrivedly in 'Die Rosenschale', magnificently in

'Archaïscher Torso Apollos'. Transferred, in *Die
Aufzeichnungen*, from the sphere of 'Ding' and 'Kunstding'
to the human sphere, it is revealed as an image of an inner,
transcendent self, self-sufficient but endowed with creative
power as agent of transformation. Raised to a mythical
level in the elegiac Angels, it subsumes within itself the
antithetical movement: the 'entströmte eigene Schönheit' is
caught back into a self-contained circle. In the ninth
Elegy it underlies the quasi-metaphysical conclusion. In
the Sonnets, it disappears. Or better, it is itself
subsumed within the image of outward movement, for the whole
Orphic sphere is self-contained in its endless flow of outward movements.

The image appears *once* in the Sonnets, in the 'sich
weigernden Schale' of the orange (SI,xv), but evaluated as
negative, as a restriction of the outward movement which is
only released in the fruit's giving of itself to the eater.
The poem concludes a sequence celebrating 'les nourritures
terrestres', and in this sequence the connexion between the
outward flow of self-giving and the fundamental theme of
assent is laid bare. The poet's stance before the Orphic
world was apprehended in the first instance as passive;
similarly, it is as receiver that man is first apprehended
as part of a universal scheme of giving:

> Selbst wenn sich der Bauer sorgt und handelt,
> wo die Saat in Sommer sich verwandelt,
> reicht er niemals hin. Die Erde *schenkt*. (SI,xii)

Between the two Sonnets on fruit is the closely associated
Sonnet on the dead, of whom it is said:

> Es ist seit lange ihre Art, den Lehm
> mit ihrem freien Marke zu durchmärken. (SI,xiv)

158

But even to receive the 'gifts' thus offered is no easy
task. Against the example of the anemone, with its 'Muskel
des unendlichen Empfangs', human receptiveness is limited:

> Wir, Gewaltsamen, wir währen länger.
> Aber *wann*, in welchem aller Leben,
> sind wir endlich offen und Empfänger? (SII,v)

For to receive fully is to give oneself; the anemones are

> manchmal *so* von Fülle übermannter,
> daß der Ruhewink des Untergangs
>
> kaum vermag die weitzurückgeschnellten
> Blätterränder dir zurückzugeben...

But the prize is also great, nothing less than the
abolition of time's destructiveness:

> Ach, das Gespenst des Vergänglichen,
> durch den arglos Empfänglichen
> geht es, als wär es ein Rauch. (SII,xxvii)

Receiving and giving are aspects of a 'Preisgegebenheit',
an assent to life-and-death, of which the death of Orpheus
is prime example:

> O wie er schwinden muß, daß ihrs begrifft!
> Und wenn es ihm selbst auch bangte, daß er
> schwände. (SI,v)

And so the Sonnets swell to celebration of that assent in
the passionate didacticism of

> Sei allem Abschied voran, als wäre er hinter
> dir, wie der Winter, der eben geht. (SII,xiii)

Assent to 'Abschied' is assent to death - 'Sei immer tot in
Eurydike' - but the injunction continues:

> ...singender steige,
> preisender steige zurück in den reinen Bezug.

'Steige' inevitably suggests Orpheus's return to earth, celebrating the knowledge he has gained from his experience of death, integrated into the totality of life-and-death:

> Sei - und wisse zugleich des Nicht-Seins Bedingung,
> den unendlichen Grund deiner innigen Schwingung,
> daß du sie völlig vollziehst dieses einzige Mal.

The last line recalls the opening of the ninth Elegy, with its emphatic '*Ein* Mal und nichtmehr', and the counter-balancing word 'Schwinden' reappears here too - but this time with a positive force:

> Hier, unter Schwindenden, sei, im Reiche der
> Neige,
> sei ein klingendes Glas, das sich im Klang schon
> zerschlug.

No image could be further removed from that of self-containment; such is the price of the resolution offered by the *Sonette an Orpheus*.

If the figure of self-containment proved so tenacious in Rilke's work, it was because it answered to a deep-rooted anxiety concerning the substantiality of the self, expressed indirectly in the nuances and paradoxes of Rilke's early work, in the tortuousness of the unrequited lover-theme and the Prodigal episode of *Malte*, and with a poignant, if universalized, directness in the second Elegy:

> ...Wie Tau von dem Frühgras
> hebt sich das Unsre von uns, wie die Hitze von
> einem
> heißen Gericht. (EII,25)

If that same figure disappears from the Sonnets, therefore, it is natural to question whether that anxiety had itself subsided. To a certain extent, the answer is already

160

apparent in the poems of 1919 and 1920, recording a transformation in Rilke's actual experience of life. And in the Sonnets, the general experience expressed in the lapidary formula 'Weils keiner meistert, bleibt das Leben rein' is developed into a sense of the mysterious *continuity* of life:

> Aber noch ist uns das Dasein verzaubert; an hundert
> Stellen ist noch Ursprung. (SII,x)

In the seventeenth Sonnet of the second part, the celebration of those 'selig bewässerten Gärten' in which grow 'die fremdartigen Früchte der Tröstung' concludes:

> Haben wir niemals vermocht, wir Schatten und
> Schemen,
> durch unser voreilig reifes und wieder welkes
> Benehmen
> jener gelassenen Sommer Gleichmut zu stören?

In the period of the poems 'Aus dem Nachlaß', this sense of continuity was clearly felt to be 'insufficient'; a mere upsurge of vital energy would not of itself answer the questioning of many years. If this same experience is worked into the Sonnets, therefore, it is only because a *framework* is now established to link it with the other major themes. At the outset of the study of Rilke's development, it was noted that one of the earliest aspirations implied by his work was that the two meanings loosely attached to the word 'Leben' - the personal sense of the self, and the greater reality of an impersonal 'élan vital' - should be merged. That merging was then short-circuited in a defensive maneouvre to safeguard the integrity of a self felt as threatened. In the Sonnets, the link is established precisely by a sense of life - in both meanings - as mysteriously continuous. Our *experience* of the inner continuity is intermittent, but it can be asserted nonetheless through its projection into the outer continuity, the sense of a wholeness without, a kind of spiritual equivalent to the conservation of matter. The answer to the elegiac lament:

> ...Schmeckt denn der Weltraum
> in dem wir uns lösen, nach uns?

is in that Sonnet with which this study opened:

> Wieviele von diesen Stellen der Räume waren schon
> innen in mir. Manche Winde
> sind wie mein Sohn.

But the answer is only possible within the context of Orphic 'Preisgegebenheit', in the same *totality* of self-abandonment which the Sonnet also celebrates. In the final Sonnet of all, assent to the *transformations* of the self is a precondition of its subsistence:

> Geh in der Verwandlung aus und ein.
> Was ist deine leidendste Erfahrung?
> Ist dir trinken bitter, werde Wein. (SII,xxix)

Rilke's choice of an assertion of the subsistence of the self as the very final words of his outbursts of February 1922, bears witness to the persistence of anxiety, *and* to a sense that he had finally found a satisfactory response to that anxiety; it answers the hope expressed in the fragment of 1912:

> Siehe, ich lebe. Woraus?

In the Sonnets, that continued subsistence of the self is predicated, not as being *despite* transience, but as being apprehended *in* transience, acceptance of which constitutes our sole guarantee:

Und wenn dich das Irdische vergaß,
zu der stillen Erde sag: Ich rinne.
Zu dem raschen Wasser sprich: Ich bin.

   *   *   *   *   *   *   *   *

In another sense, however, there is no guarantee. A
group of poems early in the first part offers a series of
gnomic formulae:

> Mag auch die Spieglung im Teich
> oft uns verschwimmen:
> *Wisse das Bild*. (SI,ix)
>
> Wissen wirs, Freunde, wissen wirs nicht?
> Beides bildet die zögernde Stunde
> in dem menschlichen Angesicht. (SI,x)
>
> Auch die sternische Verbindung trügt.
> Doch uns freue eine Weile nun
> der Figur zu glauben. Das genügt. (SI,xi)

Such admissions of nescience, in tones of such serenity,
mark a radically new note in Rilke's work. Most significant
is the third case; celebration of an ideal figure of unity
of being concludes that there is no guarantee of that unity,
but that nevertheless we have to place our faith in the
'figure' which realizes it. If that seems an enigmatic
conclusion, the following Sonnet, taking up its vocabulary,
rises to celebration:

> Heil dem Geist, der uns verbinden mag;
> denn wir leben wahrhaft in Figuren. (SI,xii)

At one level, the continuation of the Sonnet elucidates
itself as a contrast between *knowledge* and *experience*:

> Ohne unsern wahren Platz zu kennen,
> handeln wir aus wirklichem Bezug.
> Die Antennen fühlen die Antennen,
> und die leere Ferne trug...
> Reine Spannung. O Musik der Kräfte!

163

In a metaphysical sense, we are doomed to ignorance of
'unsern wahren Platz', but our experience - perhaps
intermittent, as the previous two Sonnets suggest - is
nevertheless of relatedness with the 'Musik der Kräfte'.

The word 'Kräfte' links the Sonnet with those in the
second part which celebrate the wholeness of reality. One
of those already quoted (SII,x) defines 'Dasein' as 'Ein
Spielen von reinen Kräften'; another (SII,xxvii) concludes:

> Als die, die wir sind, als die Treibenden,
> gelten wir doch bei bleibenden
> Kräften als göttlicher Brauch.

The notion of 'Figur' is thus in the first place related to
the general theme of assent; in the rhyme 'Treibenden/
bleibenden', the particular form of assent to transience is
implied. At that level, the existential realization of the
notion of 'Figur' is identical with the ground-bass of the
Orphic message:

> Wolle die Wandlung. O sei für die Flamme
>   begeistert,
> drin sich ein Ding dir entzieht, das mit
>   Verwandlungen prunkt;
> jener entwerfende Geist, welcher das Irdische
>   meistert,
> liebt in dem Schwung der Figur nichts wie den
>   wendenden Punkt. (SII,xii)

Passive assent is transcended: '*Wolle* die Wandlung...';
'Sei allem Abschied *voran*...'. This sense of active
anticipation is developed in a poem written on the eve of
the Sonnets - which also elucidates the sense of those
gnomic formulae:

> Solang du Selbstgeworfenes fängst, ist alles
> Geschicklichkeit und läßlicher Gewinn -;

erst wenn du plötzlich Fänger wirst des Balles,
den eine ewige Mitspielerin
dir zuwarf, deiner Mitte, in genau
gekonntem Schwung, in einem jener Bögen
aus Gottes großem Brücken-Bau:
erst dann ist Fangen-Können ein Vermögen, –
nicht deines, einer Welt. (II,132)

Dieter Bassermann has surmised that the poem refers to the
writing of the Sonnets – urged unexpectedly on the poet,
whereas the completion of the Elegies was a self-imposed
task.[99] The interpretation is clearly rather over-literal,
but there is a sense in which the poem points to a basic
difference between Elegies and Sonnets. The anxious
elegiac questioning – 'Habt ihr Beweise?', 'Warum denn
Menschliches müssen?' – answered ultimately by the discovery
of a task which gives 'proof', which lends meaning to human
activity, the whole sequence from 'Klage' to 'Rühmung', is
a kind of 'läßlicher Gewinn', the catching of a ball thrown
by human anxiety. Whereas the assent which governs the
Sonnets is characterized in the continuation of the poem:

> ...Und wenn du gar
> zurückzuwerfen Kraft und Mut besäßest,
> nein, wunderbarer: Mut und Kraft vergäßest
> und schon geworfen *hättest*...
>   ...erst
> in diesem Wagnis spielst du gültig mit.

For the essential difference between Elegies and Sonnets is
not between 'Klage' and 'Rühmung', nor in an unequal
proportion of the two, but in the relationship between them:

> Nur im Raum der Rühmung darf die Klage
> gehn... (SI,viii)

'Rühmung' is no longer suspended until justified by a
discovery of 'meaning'. Indeed, from this point of view the

Sonnets, no less than any previous major work of Rilke's,
represent a raising of the stakes; they incorporate into
their framework of assent a more radical critique of
'reality' - as opposed to 'Klage' concerning our relationship to that 'reality' - than anything found in the Elegies.
To return once more to that Sonnet designated by Rilke as
'gültigstes von allen', the assent is not only against a
background of mortality and transience, but against a background of an ultimate apprehension of non-being:

> Sei - und wisse zugleich des Nicht-Seins
> Bedingung,
> den unendlichen Grund deiner innigen Schwingung,
> daß du sie vollziehst dieses einzige Mal.

The last line of that tercet has already been
contrasted with the 'Ein Mal und nichtmehr' of the Elegies;
the elegiac notion of a task to be accomplished is also
taken up in the word 'vollziehst', but again with a subtle
shift of significance. In the ninth Elegy, the task was
that of transformation of the visible world, seen as
'justifying' human existence, and thereby giving it a form
of metaphysical security. Here, the transformations are *of*
the self, seen against a background of metaphysical void.
This sense of accomplishment of these figures of transformation is the burden of the two Sonnets structured
around the image of dance:

> Tänzerin: o du Verlegung
> alles Vergehens in Gang: wie brachtest du's dar.
> (SII,xviii)

In this first of the two Sonnets, the emphasis is on the
temporal dimensions of transformation, accomplishing a
resolution of movement into subsistence in the very rapidity
of transformation:

Und der Wirbel am Schluß, dieser Baum aus
Bewegung,
nahm er nicht ganz in Besitz das erschwungene
Jahr?

The use of the season-image complements the earlier Sonnet -

Denn unter Wintern ist einer so endlos Winter,
daß, überwinternd, dein Herz überhaupt übersteht. -

with the return of summer -

Blühte nicht, daß ihn dein Schwingen von vorhin
umschwärme,
plötzlich sein Wipfel von Stille? Und über ihr,
war sie nicht Sonne, war sie nicht Sommer, die
Wärme,
diese unzählige Wärme aus dir?

- and thereby brings about that 'Umkreis des ganzen
Wandelns' (EIV,61) distorted into one-sided emphasis in the
1922 retouching of the elegiac fragment.

The second Sonnet - 'an Wera', and thereby occupying a
privileged place in the cycle - also commences with the
temporal dimension in taking up once more the formula
applied to Orpheus's own recurrence: 'O komm und geh'.
But the continuation draws the theme into closer connexion
with that of 'Figur', and the celebration of ideal unity in
the hypothetical constellation as sufficient fiction:

...Du, fast noch Kind, ergänze
für einen Augenblick die Tanzfigur
zum reinen Sternbild einer jener Tänze,
darin wir die dumpf ordnende Natur
vergänglich übertreffen. (SII,xxviii)

The notion of 'figure' is in the first place assent to
those transformations which, as transient beings, we share
with the whole of creation. But it is also the means by
which we go beyond 'die dumpf ordnende Natur'; the form of
human creativity, creating the 'reines Sternbild' which we
project as image of our condition. But the two senses are

closely linked. The intuition that creative power was only possible in a condition of the self already in a certain relationship to the greater reality of 'die Erde' was one of the most tenacious threads in Rilke's work in the years preceding the Elegies. The ninth Elegy, however, reversing that intuition, made of human creativity, exercized in the transformation of the natural world, the *means* by which the self finds its existential salvation. As with other themes of those critical years, it is the Sonnets which provide the authentic resolution by re-affirming the connexion between assent to our condition and genuine creativity, and at the same time by undercutting the hankering after meta-physical certainty which proved such a powerful blockage to successful resolution in the Elegies.

One other aspect of the second dancer-sonnet is important to note at this point - the designation of the locus of authentic creativity:

> Du wußtest noch die Stelle, wo die Leier
> sich tönend hob -; die unerhörte Mitte.

The concept of a certain kind of 'centre' is an important theme in the years following completion of the Sonnets. One of the finest workings of the theme is in the 'Shawl' poem of 1923, in which the attention is focussed on

> ...die leichthin ausgespannte
> Mitte des Kaschmirshawls, die aus dem Blumensaum
> sich schwarz erneut und klärt in ihres Rahmens
> Kante
> und einen reinen Raum schafft für den Raum...

But this 'centre' is beyond 'saying':

> erfährst du dies: daß Namen sich an ihr
> endlos verschwenden: denn sie ist die Mitte.
> Wie es auch sei, das Muster unsrer Schritte,
> um eine solche Leere wandeln wir. (II,477)

A similar sense of an empty, but creative centre, is at the basis of one of the series *Im Kirchhof zu Ragaz* of 1924, in which the play of the girls around the trees is centred on the empty space,

> Und wer im Wechseln seinen Platz verlor,
> der war der Liebesgott und ohne Stelle.
>
> Die Mitte, die nach allen Seiten schreckt,
> die Wahl die zuckt, das Zücken aller Schritte-,
> und wie von Göttlicherem angesteckt,
> war jede innen beides: Baum und Mitte. (II,173)

Similarly, in 'Schwerkraft' of a few months later, gravity is defined as a form of centre:

> Mitte, wie du aus allen
> dich ziehst, auch noch aus Fliegenden dich
> wiedergewinnst, Mitte, du Stärkste. (II,179)

In this last case, the 'centre' is apprehended explicitly as the centre of a natural dynamic. But it is precisely with that natural dynamic that the ever-repeated Orphic theme 'Komm und geh' associates human experience. 'Um eine solche Leere wandeln *wir*'. In the transformations of the self in the flame of 'Wolle die Wandlung', nothing is so important as 'den wendenden Punkt'. The notion of an empty centre to the self is not new in Rilke; its most explicit formulation occurs in the course of the Prodigal episode of *Die Aufzeichnungen*, in the 'elusive, transcendent self' experienced as 'allgemein und anonym' (VI,942). There, however, the positive possibilities of the motif are threatened by a sense of emptiness as negative, as in the episode with the St Vitus's victim:

> Was hätte es für einen Sinn gehabt, noch irgendwohin
> zu gehen, ich war leer. Wie ein leeres Papier trieb
> ich an den Häusern entlang, den Boulevard wieder
> hinauf. (VI,774)

With the negative anxiety uppermost, the theme concludes
with the Prodigal's defensive gesture. In the Sonnets, it
is re-evaluated positively, and drawn into relationship with
the sense of an unknowable centre to the dynamic of the
natural world.

The particular relationship operating between the
dynamic of the natural world, and the self as dynamic
structure, both in its existential apprehension of itself
and its creative powers, is elucidated in a series of poems
of the winter of 1923 to 1924. 'Als Arbeits-Anfang eines
neuen Winters auf Muzot', Rilke wrote a dedication for
Merline, extant in two versions, classified by Zinn as
'Entwurf' and 'Vollendetes'. The first part of the poem is
substantially the same in both versions:

> Schaukel des Herzens. O sichere, an welchem
> unsichtbaren
> Aste befestigt. (II,254)

The postulation of a branch which is unknown to us, yet
which provides our security, recalls the general sense of
those poems celebrating the 'leere Mitte'. But a centre
implies a circle, and the swing travels only a half-circle;
the poem reaches out thus to the further semi-circle which
completes the whole and counterbalances the limitations of
human experience. The two versions develop this new notion
in apparently different ways. The draft turns back to those
unknown powers which first set the swing in motion:

> Aber wie sollten wir nicht, da wir nun einmal
> alles
> ihr verdanken, der ganz unvorsehlichen
> Stärke des Stoßes, glauben an jenen
> größeren Stoß, der uns ins Runde hinaufwirft?
> (II,478)

The completed version takes a different direction:

170

> ...Aber von Endpunkt zu Endpunkt
> meines gewagtesten Schwungs nehm ich ihn schon in
> Besitz:
> Überflüsse aus mir stürzen dorthin und erfülln
> ihn,
> spannen ihn fast. Und mein eigener Abschied,
> wenn die werfende Kraft an ihm abbricht,
> macht ihn mir eigens vertraut. (II,255)

The difference between the two versions - between an appeal to unknown powers and to 'Überflüsse aus mir' - echoes exactly Stephens's diagnosis, quoted earlier, of the problematic of the *Gedichte an die Nacht*, 'the question of whether the transcendent powers to which he addressed himself are an intensification and extension of something already innate in man or whether they represent something quite other and inaccessible'.[100] As was observed at that earlier point, this is the same problematic as that implied, but constantly elided, in the rapid dialectic of *Das Stundenbuch*. In the post-Sonnet period, such hesitation is not treated as problematic. For a few months later, Rilke wrote a dedication which opens:

> Wie die Natur die Wesen überläßt
> dem Wagnis ihrer dumpfen Lust und keins
> besonders schützt in Scholle und Geäst:
> so sind auch wir dem Urgrund unseres Seins
> nicht weiter lieb; *er wagt uns*. (II,261)

The notion of life as 'Wagnis' recalls 'Solang du Selbstgeworfenes fängst...', in which, however, it is *returning* the ball which is the act of daring. However, the dedication continues in precisely that direction:

> ...Nur daß wir,
> mehr noch als Pflanze oder Tier,
> *mit* diesem Wagnis gehen; es wollen; manchmal auch
> wagender sind (und nicht aus Eigennutz)
> als selbst das Leben ist -, um einen Hauch
> wagender...

171

Both the throwing of the ball and the returning are 'Wagnis'; in daring our own existences, we fulfil a universal law of daring implicit in life itself. And, to return to the 'Schaukel' poems, it is in the completed version that the notion recurs:

> Oder, wag ich es: Viertel?...

The 'Überflüsse aus mir' to which the completed version appeals are not in opposition to the 'Stärke des Stoßes' of the draft; they are an assent *to* it, 'um einen Hauch wagender' than the original 'Stoß' which sets the swing in motion.

Existentially and creatively, the self finds its salvation in assent to, but also in going beyond, the figures of transformation which are implicit in life itself; the continuity of life and of the self are apprehended through those transformations, and as *experience*, unhampered by defensiveness concerning the subsistence of the self as content, or by intransigent anxieties for meta-physical security.

Rilke's poetry subsequent to 1922 was characterized at an early stage after its publication and dating as marked by 'ein tiefes Gefühl der aus neu gefundener Geborgenheit dank-baren Lebensbejahung',[101] as bearing witness to 'a heart-catching, almost choking gratitude for the privilege of being alive'.[102] The general picture of Rilke's development which then emerged was described thus by O.F. Bollnow:

> ...die 'existentielle' Bewegung setzt ein mit dem Beginn des *Malte*, sie erreicht ihren Höhepunkt mit dem Beginn der *Duineser Elegien* im Jahre 1912 und bricht nach dem zweiten steilen Gipfel im Februar 1922 ziemlich plötzlich ab. Die vom Vertrauen zum Leben getragene Gegenbewegung dagegen setzt nach manchen leiseren Vorbereitungen in eben demselben Februar 1922 mit den *Sonetten an Orpheus* kraftvoll ein, sie erreicht

mit den erst heute in ihrem vollen Umfang bekannt
gewordenen Gedichten von 1924 ihren Höhepunkt, um dann
mit zunehmender Krankheit langsam zu verklingen.[103]

Later study, aided by deeper familiarity with the new
material, has tended to modify that view, as for instance
in Stephens's contention that

> ...one can no more speak of the serene, fulfilled and
> harmonious world of the last years than one could of
> the fulfilled and harmonious world of the *Duineser
> Elegien*. And indeed it is the Elegies, much more than
> the *Sonette an Orpheus*, which determine the over-all
> structure of the poetry of the last phase, if we take
> it as a whole and do not concentrate only on images
> of fulfilment.[104]

These two viewpoints have been quoted at length because
some general view of the shape of Rilke's career, and
particularly of the place of the *Sonette an Orpheus* within
that overall pattern, is of some importance for any assessment of the impact on Rilke's work of his reading of Valéry.
The pattern which emerges from this study is perhaps subtly,
but significantly, different from either of those proposed.

On the one hand, the radical unity of Rilke's entire
works has emerged, as determined in its broad outlines by a
concern for the nature and subsistence of the self in its
relationship to intentional objects and to the natural world
as a continuum to which the self apprehends itself as both
related and alienated. On the other hand, a specific series
of resolutions of long-matured themes has been suggested as
linking the Sonnets with later work. But that specificity
of the late work has not been defined, as both Bollnov and
Stephens imply - one in asserting, the other in denying -
in terms of elegiac 'Klage' and Orphic 'Rühmung', at least
not in any straightforward sense. The experience of life
expressed by the late work is implicit in much of Rilke's

work from the very beginning, both as 'Klage' for the
limitations of the human condition, and as 'Rühmung' for
what is nonetheless possible. If it is possible to identify
periods of Rilke's *life* marked by negative and positive
moods, then the lowest point appears to be in the immediate
pre-war years, the highest immediately after. Both
experiences find their way into the *Duineser Elegien*. What
matters - and what clearly mattered *to Rilke* - was the
creation of a framework which would express both without
self-contradiction. And it is in this light that the
specific success of the Sonnets should be recognized. It
has been repeatedly observed that there is nothing
positively new in the *Sonette an Orpheus*; the preconditions
of their resolutions are rather certain *renunciations*, the
abandonment of a certain defensive image of the self, and
the abandonment of the urge to create an all-embracing
quasi-metaphysical *system*. One or other, or both, of these,
can be seen as blocking mechanisms which inhibited successful resolution of themes as old as *Die Frühen Gedichte* - in
Das Stundenbuch, in *Die Aufzeichnungen des Malte Laurids
Brigge*, and in the ninth and tenth *Duineser Elegien*.

Whether, if Rilke had lived longer, the *Sonette an
Orpheus* would have appeared as his 'final word' in terms of
full-scale cycles is of course entirely hypothetical. In
certain of the poems of 1925 there are signs that he might
have entered upon an entirely new phase with markedly
different concerns; if that promise had been fulfilled, it
would only substantiate the 'finality' of the *Sonette an
Orpheus*, not as creating a definitive 'system', but as
finally laying to rest, not 'Klage' for the human condition,
but certain persistent anxieties. As it is, the work of the
years 1922 to 1925 is disparate and inconclusive in terms of
new directions. But there is no return to the insistent
anxieties of the *Buch von der Armut und vom Tode* or *Das Buch*

der Bilder, to the trough of despair of 1915, or to the bleak-
ness of the tenth Elegy. Even the anguished and intensely
moving final draft, 'Komm du, du letzter, den ich anerkenne'
(II,511) has nothing of the *defensiveness* of those earlier
low-points. And his final completed poem - the conclusion,
written within a few months of death, to the correspondence
with Erika Mitterer - is one of his most accomplished
expressions of danger drawn into assent, of acceptance of
'des Nicht-Seins Bedingung' into a totality of experience,
of 'Wagnis' become 'Sichersein':

> Taube, die draußen blieb,   außer dem Taubenschlag,
> wieder in Kreis und Haus,   einig der Nacht, dem
> Tag,
> weiß sie die Heimlichkeit,   wenn sich der Einbezug
> fremdester Schrecken schmiegt   in den gefühlten
> Flug.
>
> Unter den Tauben, die   allergeschonteste,
> niemals gefährdetste,   kennt nicht die Zärtlich-
> keit;
> wiedererholtes Herz   ist das bewohnteste:
> freier durch Widerruf   freut sich die Fähigkeit.
>
> Über dem Nirgendssein   spannt sich das Überall!
> Ach der geworfene,   ach der gewagte Ball,
> füllt er die Hände nicht   anders mit Wiederkehr:
> rein um sein Heimgewicht   ist er mehr. (II,319)

VIII. CONCLUSION

Rilke and Valéry were without doubt the greatest poets of their generation in their respective languages. That this is so makes the encounter between them all the more remarkable. At the same time, Valéry's *stature* as poet is of course itself part of the explanation for Rilke's enthusiasm, an aspect of his example which should not be ignored for being self-evident. In his post-war exile in Switzerland, Rilke was isolated not only by geography and by a war which had broken many links; he was isolated simply as a poet, as - in Hölderlin's phrase - 'Dichter in dürftiger Zeit'. He had recognized the genius of Mann in 1902, of Gide in 1908, of Proust in 1913 and of Kafka in 1914, but the listing of four novelists bears witness to an acuteness of discrimination that could not fail to make him aware of the precariousness of his situation as poet. Hofmannsthal has ceased writing long ago; Trakl, in whom Rilke had seen 'eine neue Dimension des geistigen Raums',[105] had been removed by war; from George he had always preserved a defensive distance;[106] and for post-war Expressionism he had little taste. As for the French, it was not to be supposed that the gentle lyricism of Francis Jammes or Anna de Noailles, though their work might provide evidence of a continuity disrupted in Germany by the crisis of Expressionism and the Great War, could suggest a distinguished role for poetry in the post-war world. 'Nous autres, civilisations, nous savons maintenant que nous sommes mortelles', had been Valéry's reaction to the War (I,988);

and for Rilke, despite his eclectic interest in other
literary forms and other arts, poetry *was* civilization.
Even from their opening lines, 'Le Cimetière marin' and
La Jeune Parque (whose classical Alexandrines Valéry saw as
a final monument to a doomed culture) could not but evoke a
response, whatever their concerns in terms of subject-matter
and themes, as evidence of a major poet at work, and at work
neither as epigone of a bygone age nor as purveyor of self-
conscious novelty - as evidence that

> Zwischen den Hämmern besteht
> unser Herz, wie die Zunge
> zwischen den Zähnen, die doch,
> dennoch, die preisende bleibt.

It is in this context in the first place that the
remarkably similar patterns of the two poets' careers (to
the date of their encounter) should be placed. That 'grand
silence' to which Rilke so passionately, and so naturally,
responded, is an indication of a certain kind of radicalism
which was Rilke's also and which was the condition of the
greatness of both poets. Not of a fashionable kind of
radicalism - Valéry recalls the seventeenth century in the
age of nascent Surrealism, and Rilke is not a 'modernist'
poet set beside Stramm - but of a radicalism which rejected
compromise and premature syntheses, which led Rilke to
repudiate the whole of his earliest work and embark on a
career characterized by a determined and progressive raising
of the stakes, which led Valéry to repudiate poetry until he
could match the overwhelming example of Mallarmé - 'seule
tête - hors de prix! - à couper, pour décapiter toute Rome'
(I,1729), a radicalism which permitted neither the
impressionist exploitation of lyrical commonplace nor an
easy ride on the more dramatic currents of the time,
Expressionist or vitalist.

But in *La Jeune Parque* - or in 'Le Cimetière marin', if
that was his introduction to Valéry - Rilke found not only
an exemplary demonstration of the continuing possibility of
poetry; he found also dramas which exploited a tension basic
to his own work, a tension most succinctly defined as being
between 'open' and 'closed' views of the self. But if that
tension was Rilke's own, he found it presented in Valéry's
work - to look first at the handling of certain crucial
images - in a different light. In his own work, he had
striven towards a synthesis of images of a total 'open-ness'
towards reality, and of a closed self-containment; that
synthesis he had achieved only by the invocation of
'Gestorbensein', by the nuances and paradoxes of the closed
but all-embracing circle of the unrequited lover, or by
transference to a transcendental plane in the angelic
consciousness. In 'Le Cimetière marin', he found that
synthesis achieved in the association of the dead with the
absolute circularity and self-sufficiency, the 'parfait
diadème' of 'Midi' - and then energetically repudiated,
along with all aspiration to transcendence, in the
conclusion that the 'absolute' condition of the dead was
best left to the dead. Rilke admired in Valéry the
suppression of 'toutes les formes provisoires';[107] elements
elaborated in his own work over many years in a complex
texture of images, reformulated, re-evaluated and nuanced,
he found presented in 'Le Cimetière marin' with the directness of Valéry's elemental imagery of sun and sea, and with
an appearance of uncompromising *finality*.

Yet however inexorable the poetic logic of a poem such
as 'Le Cimetière marin', there was nothing harsh or pitiless
about the works of Valéry. Where Rilke's despair led him in
1915, and again in 1922 in the tenth Elegy, to bitter
excoriation of humanity, the young Fate, from the depths of
her despair, cries

J'ai pitié de nous tous, ô tourbillons de poudre!
and finds an exit from her impasse in the 'allzumenschliches'
of a tear. At the emergence from her night of drama, rather
than simply dismissing it as inconclusive, she accepts the
reconciliation offered by the light; and in emerging from
the monumental labours of *La Jeune Parque*, Valéry provided,
in the three *Odes*, an object-lesson in balance and mutual
consent between the warring partners within the self.

Rilke had come near to a similar position in 1912, in
the first two Elegies. Built into them is a realization of
the impossibility of achieving within the living human
consciousness the synthesis of absolute open-ness and closed
self-sufficiency which is the definition of the angelic
condition, and in their closing lines is implicit a
renunciation of any direct annexation of the condition of
the dead. But from this point the two poets moved in very
different directions, and these directions are indicative of
one deep and abiding dissimilarity between them. For
Valéry, poet only intermittently, poetry itself, though the
'exercise' *par excellence* in which human experience could be
given lasting shape, was only one mode of discourse among
others, and the one in which this least systematic of
thinkers was least inclined to come to systematic
conclusions. The internal dramas which lay behind the
finished forms of the poetry could be minutely dissected
elsewhere, the more extreme forms of internal possibility
analysed in other forms of discourse, leaving poetry the
task only of representing patterns of resolution of those
dramas, returns from those extremities. For Rilke, though
he satisfied his need for more explicit discourse in one of
the most voluminous of any poet's correspondences, poetry
was ultimately the only stage for his internal dramas, on
which all extremities and every abortive resolution had to
be played out. And for him, conclusions *were* to be reached;

though his constant awareness of 'des andern Aufwand'
allowed time and time again only a precarious point of
balance, subsequently dismissed as unsatisfactory or
incomplete, nevertheless behind all his work is an urge to
conclude - not only to give a total account of the
condition of modern man, but to give an account which led
from lament to total triumph. Faced with the necessity
of completing the *Duineser Elegien* on pain of admitting
defeat in the task they announce from the outset, that urge
proved overwhelming; having sketched out partially
incompatible premisses and conclusions, and having in some
sense already gone beyond those 'conclusions', he fell back
into repetition of earlier, abortive resolutions, with an
anxious withdrawal of all creative power into a 'closed'
self, and a further invocation of 'Gestorbensein' as image
of absolute 'open-ness', the two only synthesized on a
transcendental plane in the pseudo-metaphysics of the
Hulewicz letter. From *his* major works of critical
extremity, Valéry moved towards the short poems of *Charmes*,
whose formal achievement mirrors the realization of a self
living without anxiety in a balanced tension accepted as
necessary and fruitful.

Rilke did finally achieve something akin to the balance
of 'Les Pas', in the 'Gegengewicht, in dem ich mich
rhythmisch ereigne' of the *Sonette an Orpheus*. And it is
time - though not as the very final perspective on the
'Rilke-Valéry question' - to attempt to provide an account
of those features of the Sonnets which seem to suggest an
answering echo to those major works of Valéry read, copied
and translated in the twelve months before composition.

A schematic account of Valéry's apprehension of the
self as found in those works analysed would be as follows.
Consciousness aspires by its very nature to a paradoxical

synthesis of uniqueness and universality; it is a movement
of withdrawal and self-closure which, if it could be
completed, would result in an exclusive circularity seen as
a form of transcendence. But this transcendence is
literally impossible; there is no 'closure' for consciousness, which is enchained to its incarnation in a total
structure of the self as living entity, whose continuity
escapes definition, and can only be grasped *a posteriori*.
The self as a whole is apprehended only in becoming, not
in being, as a rhythm of exchange, but as a rhythm organized
around a central invariant, itself 'empty': form rather than
content, capacity for transformation rather than result of
any specific transformation. These transformations themselves, experienced at one level as a 'porosity' of
sensibility to the external world, link the self at that
level to the organic transformations of life, and both self
and world are apprehended by the creative imagination as
parallel dynamic figurations, relationships rather than
entities. Existentially, therefore, the remedy for the
inability of the self to pass a certain threshold and seize
itself as pure being, lies in the acceptance of indefinite
re-commencement, each new departure bearing witness to the
absolute virtuality of the organizing centre of the self as
pure negativity. The creative imagination, caught within
the closed sphere of a Universe which it knows as ultimately
random, a contingent series of forms which could be otherwise, affirms its awareness of that contingency in the
creation of form as a certain 'excess' over the purely
given.

In the *Sonette an Orpheus*, Rilke renounces a form of
transcendence implied in an image of the self as self-
contained source of creative power, affirmed in its closure.
That closure operated as a defence against an apprehension
of the self as dissipation, and is overtaken in an

apprehension of life itself as a series of transformations
which yet result in an inexplicable continuity; the self
finds its subsistence therefore in association with that
continuity rather than in a defence of its own permanence, in
the acceptance of the self as a series of transformations by
which an experience of reality as figurations organized
around an 'empty' centre is *accomplished*. Creativity is not
an Archimedean point from which the self is affirmed as
assured of an independent standpoint outside the sphere of
life itself, but as the 'Wagnis' which goes beyond
experience of intermittence to completed figures of the
dynamic of life.

What is principally required to transform the account
of Valéry's sense of the self into an account of the underlying structure of the *Sonette an Orpheus* is an
intensification of *tone*, the addition of a higher charge of
existential necessity to Valéry's sometimes abstract
formulae. This change of tone constitutes that revisionary
'Steigerung' noted at the outset in the contrast of 'Les
Pas' with 'Atmen, du unsichtbares Gedicht'; it bears witness
to the greater depths of Rilke's anxiety concerning the
self, and conversely, to a continuing need to postulate an
ontological substantiality to the continuum of 'life'. But
the difference may after all be one of discourse rather than
substance. 'Life', whether viewed in a spirit of analytic
detachment (as in Valéry's abstract meditations) or as a
greater reality 'without' (as in Rilke's discourse of pantheistic transcendence), is ultimately something
experienced, and experienced *immanently*.

'J'attendais. Toute mon oeuvre attendait. Un jour,
j'ai lu Valéry, j'ai su que mon attente était finie.' It
seems impossible to interpret Rilke's confession as implying
that Valéry's works provided in any sense the 'key' to

completion of the *Duineser Elegien*. As has been observed -
not by any means for the first time in Rilke literature -
the 'message' of the 1922 Elegies depended on no new
revelation. But the phrase 'toute mon oeuvre' can be
interpreted in a more general way; all Rilke's work - his
total 'oeuvre' - had tended towards a certain form of
resolution which it finds in fully-elaborated form only in
the *Sonette an Orpheus*. In the work of Valéry, Rilke
found no new elements, but a structure remarkably similar
to that which was latent, 'waiting', in his own work, and
one presented always against the backcloth of a renunciation,
analogous to the renunciation which *was* the key to that
resolution.

In a certain sense, therefore, the example of Valéry's
work for Rilke was negative. But it can perhaps be re-
defined in more positive terms. Rilke-criticism has been
much occupied of recent years with the possibility of
defining the historicity of his work. That question has been
approached mainly through the implied aesthetics of his
later works, and much of value has been said on the subject.
This study has concentrated on the primarily existential
concerns of Rilke's poetry, bearing in mind his own statement
that

> so sehr der Künstler in einem auch das *Werk* meint,
> ...ganz gerecht wird man erst, wenn man einsieht,
> daß auch diese dringendste Realisierung einer
> höhern Sichtbarkeit...nur als Mittel erscheint,
> einen heileren Zustand in der Mitte des eigenen
> Wesens zu gewinnen.[108]

But the existential dimension which has been emphasized in
these pages may be itself a possible way of approaching
Rilke's historical situation, especially in the light of
comparison with Valéry.

In the works of both poets, the theme of the self is inextricably linked with that of time, and at one level that theme provides one of the most fundamental of contrasts between them. For Rilke, time presents itself most naturally in terms of the relationship between past and present, in the historical contrasts always to the detriment of the present, or at a more fundamental level in the evaluation of 'Erinnerung' as 'Er-innerung'. At the same time, escape from 'durée' as dissipation is predicated on a certain sense of futurity:

> ...Wie kann
> das Geringste geschehn, wenn nicht die Fülle der
> Zukunft,
> alle vollzählige Zeit, sich uns entgegenbewegt?
> (II,42)

In *La Jeune Parque*, Valéry plunges into the labyrinthine relationship between past and present, but concludes with recognition of the 'doux et puissant retour du délice de naître'; 'Le Cimetière marin' escapes from the apparent immobilization of the present into the futurity of 'l'ère successive':

> L'idée du passé ne prend un sens et ne constitue
> une valeur que pour l'homme qui se trouve en soi-
> même une *passion de l'avenir*. (II,917)

Only in the *Sonette an Orpheus* does Rilke consistently celebrate futurity. Acceptance of transience is modulated into an overtaking: '*Wolle* die Wandlung...', 'Sei allem Abschied *voran*...'. The experience of existential continuity in the poems of 1919 and 1920 is intensified into a sense of endless renewal: 'an hundert Stellen ist noch Ursprung'. Even the conservative task of the seventh and ninth Elegies is transcended:

Wir, ein Geschlecht durch Jahrtausende: Mütter und
                                                Väter,
    immer erfüllter von dem künftigen Kind...
                                            (SII,xxiv)

In the introduction to his *Études sur le temps humain*,
Georges Poulet characterizes the post-Romantic sense of time
as 'un profond sentiment d'usure', as the impossibility of
creating 'un être dans la durée' except intermittently by
'la brève flambée de la mémoire affective'.[109] The passage
to a characteristically twentieth-century apprehension of the
self in time is marked by Bergson's re-definition of
'devenir' from 'être changé' to 'changer', bearing witness to

> le sentiment que n'importe quel moment peut être vécu
> comme un moment neuf, et que le temps peut être
> toujours créé librement à partir du moment présent.[110]

Access to this 'création continue', however, is only through
an 'act of annihilation':

> Si l'esprit veut se saisir comme créateur, ...il faut
> qu'il fasse son propre néant pour se donner un être.[111]

In attempting to define Rilke's literary-historical situation
Anthony Stephens concludes that there are Rimbaldian and
Mallarméan elements in his work, to be seen as partially
conflicting elements.[112] But seen from a sufficiently wide
perspective, the Rimbaud-Mallarmé opposition dissolves into
affinity as a liquidation of the passivity inherent in
Romantic transcendentalism:

> C'est à partir du néant mallarméen que se font la
> création gidienne de l'instant et la création
> valérienne du temps; c'est à partir de l'innocence
> rimbaldienne que se fait la création surréaliste d'un
> sur-instant ou d'une sur-durée.[113]

Rilke's own 'modernity' has often been in doubt. From this

particular perspective, the *Sonette an Orpheus* represent
Rilke's passage into modernity - achieved,
characteristically, not so much by a liquidation of
Romanticism as by a nuancing to vanishing point. It is not
only in their subtly altered sense of time that the Sonnets
attain such a modernity, but also in their awareness of 'le
néant', not as threat - as 'Grund von Gegenteil' - but as a
form of 'innocence', as the basis of that 'Wagnis' which, in
going ahead of knowledge derived from experience, creates
the world afresh. This sense of a void as springboard for
departure links the Rilke of the Sonnets with the major
figures of European modernism in the Anglo-French mould,
with Proust and Joyce as well as with Valéry. (The latter's
misunderstanding of the essential nature of Proust's
'recherche du temps perdu' is blatant, and the frequently
drawn contrast of Valéry and Bergson depends on elements in
Bergson's later works which take him progressively away from
'les données immédiates de la conscience'.[114]) The founding
fathers of modern sensibility share a profound sense of the
infinite *possibilities* of life, of

> The way the earliest single light in the evening
> sky,
> Creates a fresh universe out of nothingness...115

And it is perhaps in this perspective that the example of
Valéry on Rilke's work should be seen. Given the extent to
which each single element of the total structure of the
Sonette an Orpheus can be traced back into earlier work, it
is in this reconfiguration of already familiar features into
a forward-moving rather than conservative or atemporal
structure that the impact of the French poet's work should
be located.

But that impact is unimaginable without the total

context in which it has been placed in this study. The re-
use of certain borrowed images of flame and dance - to
return to the starting-point - is a trivial matter unless
it is seen in relation to the much wider, more diffuse
influence which the reading of Valéry's work appears to
have had on Rilke's re-ordering of his poetic world in the
Sonnets. But that influence was itself without doubt
conditional on the sense of affinity which this study has
principally set out to elucidate. As was observed earlier,
any account of Valéry's influence in the Sonnets has to bear
in mind the possibility of other sources. To take the case
of 'Wolle die Wandlung', for example - *locus classicus* for
earlier discussions of Rilke and Valéry - one could add to
Heller's Nietzschean interpretation the obvious comparison
with Goethe's 'Selige Sehnsucht':

> Sagt es niemand, nur den Weisen,
> Weil die Menge gleich verhöhnet,
> Das Lebendge will ich preisen,
> Das nach Flammentod sich sehnet...
>
> Und so lang du das nicht hast,
> Dieses: Stirb und werde!
> Bist du nur ein trüber Gast
> Auf der dunklen Erde.

The history of Rilke's relationships with his great
predecessors, with Hölderlin as well as Goethe, remains to
be written in its full depth. It would no doubt be a
largely subterranean history; for any subsequent German
poet, the influence of either could only be, in Harold
Bloom's terms, a form of anxiety.[116] Eudo Mason has
analysed the extent to which Rodin operated as 'George-
substitute' for Rilke, as substitute for an influence which
could not be directly acknowledged.[117] If Rilke's work is
held open more readily to Nietzsche, it is because
Nietzsche was not principally a poet. Valéry was a poet -
but a foreign one. And it is without doubt significant

that, however much 'Wolle die Wandlung' echoes Nietzsche
and Goethe, it was with *L'Ame et la danse* in mind - the
entire dialogue written out in his own hand only a few weeks
before - that Rilke wrote the Sonnet.

But the more important point is that both dialogue and
Sonnet represent resolutions of structural tensions in the
entire works of their authors. The condition of the
influence of *L'Ame et la danse* on the *Sonette an Orpheus* was
the impact, in the widest sense, of Valéry's works on Rilke,
the total *example* of Valéry, located in Rilke's intuitive
grasp, behind the finished forms of the poems and dialogues,
of existential anxieties, projects and manoeuvres which
echoed his own experience.

In a sense, the question *is* one of language - but not
in the sense of style, and not primarily from Rilke's point
of view - though Valéry's ability to move easily between
different modes of discourse was indirectly a cause of
Rilke's admiration for the authoritative finality of the
works he read. It is for the third party, reader or critic -
or critic as 'reader' - that the question of forms of discourse is all-important. Whatever the complex mechanisms of
influence and revision may have been which produced the
texts, the texts are there, and invite interpretation.
Interpretation of literary texts is not a reductive decod-
ing, but a translation - from one language into another, the
second less rich and continuous, but more explicit and
abstract than the first. The opportunity offered by
comparison, when sanctioned by an encounter such as that in
question here, is that of taking as starting-point, in
attempting to grasp and articulate the fundamental human
experience woven into the texts, not one, but two richly
elaborated and resonant discourses.

NOTES

(Full bibliographical details of works referred to in the
Notes are to be found in the Bibliography which follows.)

1. The most recent and thorough accounts are to be found
   in: Charles Dédéyan, *Rilke et la France*, and Karin
   Wais, *Rilkes Valéry-Übertragungen*.

2. Claire Goll, *Rilke et les femmes*, p. 24.

3. Monique St. Hélier, 'Souvenir', in *Rilke et la France*,
   p. 233.

4. *Correspondance, Rainer Maria Rilke et Merline*, p. 186.

5. *ibid.*, p. 278.

6. *Correspondance, Rainer Maria Rilke et André Gide*, p. 151.

7. *Briefwechsel, Rainer Maria Rilke und Katherina Kippenberg*, pp. 570-71.

8. *Correspondance, Rainer Maria Rilke et André Gide*, p. 162.

9. *ibid.*, p. 168.

10. *Briefwechsel, Rainer Maria Rilke und Maria von Thurn und
    Taxis-Hohenlohe*, II,686.

11. *Correspondance, Rainer Maria Rilke et André Gide*, p. 176,
    and *Correspondance, Rainer Maria Rilke et Merline*,
    pp. 383 and 387.

12. *Correspondance, Rainer Maria Rilke et André Gide*,
    pp. 179-80.

13. *Correspondance, Rainer Maria Rilke et Merline*, p. 394.

14. *ibid.*, p. 385.

15. *ibid.*, p. 399.

16. Karin Wais, *Rilkes Valéry-Übertragungen*, p. 17.

17. *Briefe aus Muzot*, p. 124.

18. See von Salis, *Rilkes Schweizer Jahre*, Part 4, Chapter
    1.

19. *Briefwechsel, Rainer Maria Rilke und Maria von Thurn
    und Taxis-Hohenlohe*, II, 734.

20. *Briefe aus Muzot*, p. 157.

21. *Briefwechsel, Rainer Maria Rilke und Katherina Kippen-
    berg*, p. 482.

22. *ibid.*, p. 495. See also *Correspondance, Rainer Maria
    Rilke et Merline*, p. 426.

23. Quoted in Renée Lang, *Rilke, Gide et Valéry*, p. 45.

24. *Briefwechsel, Rainer Maria Rilke und Maria von Thurn und
    Taxis-Hohenlohe*, II,802.

25. Maurice Betz, *Rilke à Paris*. The personal relationship between the two poets is discussed in Karin Wais, *Rilkes Valéry-Übertragungen*, pp. 10-14.

26. Published in *Entretiens sur Paul Valéry*, facing p. 337.

27. *Briefwechsel, Rainer Maria Rilke und Katherina Kippenberg*, p. 569.

28. *Briefe an seinen Verleger*, p. 452.

29. *ibid.*, p. 454. See also *Briefe an Frau Gudi Nölke*, pp. 132 and 201.

30. *Correspondance, Rainer Maria Rilke et Merline*, pp. 602-03.

31. For details, see Karin Wais, *Rilkes Valéry-Übertragungen*, pp. 15-22.

32. Hartmann Goertz, *Frankreich und das Erlebnis der Form im Werke Rainer Maria Rilkes*, p. 91.

33. Marga Bauer, *Rainer Maria Rilke und Frankreich*, p. 74.

34. *ibid.*, p. 69.

35. J.F. Angelloz, *Rilke*, p. 289.

36. Charles Dédéyan, *Rilke et la France*; K.A.J. Batterby, *Rilke and France. A Study in Poetic Development.*

37. K.A.J. Batterby, *Rilke and France*, pp. 192-193.

38. J.R. von Salis, *Rainer Maria Rilkes Schweizer Jahre*, p. 144.

39. Renée Lang, *Rilke, Gide et Valéry*, p. 23.

40. K.A.J. Batterby, *Rilke and France*, p. 153.

41. Charles Dédéyan, *Rilke et la France*, IV, 346.

42. See E.L. Stahl, *Rainer Maria Rilkes 'Duineser Elegien'*, p. 32.

43. Charles Dédéyan, *Rilke et la France*, IV, 348-49.

44. See Marga Bauer, *Rainer Maria Rilke und Frankreich*, pp. 66-67.

45. Erich Heller, *The Disinherited Mind*, pp. 112-13.

46. Hartmann Goertz, *Frankreich und das Erlebnis der Form im Werke Rainer Maria Rilkes*, p. 86.

47. Dietgard Kramer-Lauff, *Tanz und Tänzerisches in Rilkes Lyrik.*

48. Geoffrey Hartman, *The Unmediated Vision: An Interpretation of Wordsworth, Hopkins, Rilke and Valéry.*

49. Priscilla Washburn Shaw, *Rilke, Valéry and Yeats: The Domain of the Self.*

50. Geoffrey Hartman, *The Unmediated Vision*, p. 156.

51. J.R. Lawler, *Lecture de Valéry: Une Étude de 'Charmes'*, pp. 78-82.

52. *Cahiers*, XXVIII,427.

53. In *Dernière visite à Mallarmé* (I, 630 ff.).

54. Christine M. Crow, *Paul Valéry: Consciousness and Nature*, p. 8.

55. P.W. Shaw, *Rilke, Valéry and Yeats*, p. 118.

56. J.B. Leishman, *Rainer Maria Rilke: 'Sonnets to Orpheus'*, p. 162.

57. F.W. van Heerikhuizen, *Rainer Maria Rilke: His Life and Works*, p. 95.

58. Frank Wood, *Rainer Maria Rilke: The Ring of Forms*, p. 20.

59. Eudo C. Mason, *Rilke*, p. 27.

60. Käte Hamburger, 'Die phänomenologische Struktur der Dichtung Rilkes', in *Rilke in neuer Sicht*, pp. 83-158.

61. *ibid.*, p. 110.

62. Eudo C. Mason, *Rilke*, p. 48.

63. R.D. Laing, *The Divided Self*, p. 45.

64. *ibid.*, p. 69.

65. *ibid.*, p. 44.

66. *ibid.*, p. 88.

67. 'Profusion du Soir', printed in the *Album*, is probably much later in date than the others. See J.R. Lawler, *The Poet as Analyst: Essays on Paul Valéry*, pp. 74-116, and Hartmut Köhler, *Paul Valéry: Dichtung und Erkenntnis*, pp. 102-04.

68. Marcel Raymond, *Paul Valéry et la tentation de l'esprit*, p. 11.

69. *ibid.*, p. 11.

70. *ibid.*, p. 13.

71. Hartmut Köhler, *Paul Valéry: Dichtung und Erkenntnis*, p. 29 (*Cahiers*, IV,351).

72. *ibid.*, p. 34 (*Cahiers*, IV, 181).

73. F.D. Luke, 'Metaphor and Thought in Rilke's *Duino Elegies*', *Oxford German Studies*, 2 (1967), 124.

74. Jacob Steiner, *Rilkes Duineser Elegien*, p. 53.

75. Anthony Stephens, *Rainer Maria Rilke's 'Gedichte an die Nacht'*.

76. *ibid.*, p. 38.

77. *ibid.*, p. 40.

78. Dieter Bassermann, *Der späte Rilke*, pp. 49ff.

79. Anthony Stephens, *Rainer Maria Rilke's 'Gedichte an die Nacht'*, pp. 80-83.

80. Dieter Bassermann, *Der späte Rilke*, pp. 354-55.

81. E.L. Stahl, *Rainer Maria Rilke's 'Duineser Elegien'*, p. 34.

82. *ibid.*, p. xxx.

83. *ibid.*, p. xxxiv.

84. L.G. Salingar, 'T.S. Eliot: Poet and Critic', in *Pelican Guide to English Literature*, VII, 347.

85. E.L. Stahl, *Rainer Maria Rilke's 'Duineser Elegien'*, p. ix.

86. Jacob Steiner, *Rilkes Duineser Elegien*.

87. E.L. Stahl, *Rainer Maria Rilke's 'Duineser Elegien'*, p. ix.

88. Käte Hamburger, 'Die phänomenologische Struktur der Dichtung Rilkes', in *Rilke in neuer Sicht*, p. 149.

89. Romano Guardini, *Rainer Maria Rilkes Deutung des Daseins*.

90. F.D. Luke, 'Metaphor and Thought in Rilke's *Duino Elegies*', *Oxford German Studies*, 2 (1967), 113.

91. Käte Hamburger, 'Die phänomenologische Struktur der Dichtung Rilkes', in *Rilke in neuer Sicht*, p. 123.

92. Jean Hytier, 'Étude de *La Jeune Parque*', in *Questions de littérature*, p. 3.

93. Marcel Raymond, *Paul Valéry et la tentation de l'esprit*, p. 120.

94. Geoffrey Hartman, *The Unmediated Vision*, p. 107.

95. Jean Levaillant, 'La Jeune Parque en question', in *Paul Valéry contemporain*, pp. 137-52.

96. *ibid.*, pp. 143-44.

97. J.R. Lawler, *Lecture de Valéry: Une Étude de 'Charmes'* p. 211.

98. Christine M. Crow, *Paul Valéry: Consciousness and Nature*, p. 4.

99. Dieter Bassermann, *Der späte Rilke*, pp. 385-86.

100. Anthony Stephens, *Rainer Maria Rilke's 'Gedichte an die Nacht'*, p. 40.

101. O.F. Bollnow, *Rilke*, p. 345.

102. J.B. Leishman, *Rainer Maria Rilke: Poems 1906 to 1926*, p. 54.

103. O.F. Bollnow, *Rilke*, pp. 313-14.

104. Anthony Stephens, 'The Problem of Completeness in Rilke's Poetry, 1922-26', *Oxford German Studies*, 4 (1969), 185.

105. Quoted by Beda Allemann, *Zeit und Figur beim späten Rilke*, p. 301.

106. See Eudo C. Mason, 'Rilke und Stefan George', in *Rilke in neuer Sicht*, pp. 9-37.

107. *Correspondance, Rainer Maria Rilke et André Gide*, p. 151.

108. Quoted O.F. Bollnow, *Rilke*, Chapter 19.

109. Georges Poulet, *Études sur le temps humain*, p. 43.

110. *ibid.*, p. 45.

111. *ibid.*, p. 46.

112. Anthony Stephens, *Rilke's 'Gedichte an die Nacht'*, p. 225.

113. Georges Poulet, *Études sur le temps humain*, pp. 46-47.

114. See, for example, Christine Crow, *Paul Valéry: Consciousness and Nature*, p. 228.

115. Wallace Stevens, *Collected Poems*, p. 517.

116. Harold Bloom, *The Anxiety of Influence. A Theory of Poetry*.

117. Eudo C. Mason, 'Rilke and Stefan George', in *Rilke in neuer Sicht*, pp. 9-37.

BIBLIOGRAPHY

A. WORKS AND LETTERS OF RILKE

Sämtliche Werke, edited by Ernst Zinn, 6 vols (Wiesbaden/Frankfurt am Main, 1955-67).

Briefe aus Muzot 1921 bis 1926 (Leipzig, 1936).

Briefwechsel, Rainer Maria Rilke und Katherina Kippenberg (Wiesbaden, 1954).

Die Briefe an Frau Gudi Nölke aus Rilkes Schweizer Jahre (Wiesbaden, 1953).

Briefwechsel, Rainer Maria Rilke und Lou Andreas-Salomé (Zürich/Wiesbaden, 1952).

Briefwechsel, Rainer Maria Rilke und Marie von Thurn und Taxis-Hohenlohe, 2 vols (Zürich/Wiesbaden, 1951).

Briefe an seinen Verleger 1906 bis 1926 (Leipzig, 1934).

Correspondance, Rainer Maria Rilke et André Gide 1906-1926 (Paris, 1952).

Correspondance, Rainer Maria Rilke et Merline (Zürich, 1954).

B. WORKS OF VALÉRY

Oeuvres, edited by J. Hytier, 2 vols (Paris, 1957, 1960).

Cahiers, vols. I-XXIX (Paris, 1957-1961).

C. WORKS ON RILKE

Allemann, Beda, *Zeit und Figur beim späten Rilke. Ein Beitrag zur Poetik des modernen Gedichtes* (Pfullingen, 1961).

Angelloz, J.F., *Rilke* (Paris, 1961).

Angelloz, J.F., 'Rilke traducteur de Valéry', *Cahiers de l'Association internationale des études françaises*, 8 (1956), 107-112.

Bassermann, Dieter, *Der späte Rilke*, second edition (Essen/Freiburg-im-Breisgau, 1948).

Batterby, K.A.J., *Rilke and France. A Study in Poetic Development* (London, 1966).

Bauer, Marga, *Rainer Maria Rilke und Frankreich* (Bern 1931).

Behrendt, Hans, *Rainer Maria Rilkes Neue Gedichte. Versuch einer Deutung* (Bonn, 1957).

Belmore, H.W., *Rilke's Craftsmanship. An Analysis of his poetic style* (Oxford, 1966).

Bémol, Maurice, 'Rilke et les influences', *Revue de littérature comparée*, 27 (1953), 169-181.

Bémol, Maurice, 'Rilke et Valéry', in *Variations sur Valéry*, (Paris, 1959), II, 159-74.

Betz, Maurice, *Rilke à Paris* (Paris, 1941).

Betz, Maurice, 'Valéry et Rilke.', in *Paul Valéry vivant* (Marseille, 1946).

Bollnow, O.F., *Rilke*, second edition (Stuttgart, 1956).

Bowra, Maurice, *The Heritage of Symbolism* (London, 1942).

Buddeberg, Else, *Rainer Maria Rilke. Eine innere Biographie* (Stuttgart, 1955).

Butler, E.M., *Rainer Maria Rilke*, second edition (Cambridge, 1946).

Casey, Timothy, *Rainer Maria Rilke. A Centenary Essay* (London, 1976).

Clery, A.R. de, *Rilke traducteur* (Geneva, 1956).

Crasnow, Ellman, 'Poems and Fictions. Stevens, Rilke, Valéry', in *Modernism 1890-1930*, edited by Malcolm Bradbury and James McFarlane (London, 1976).

Dédéyan, Charles, *Rilke et la France*, 4 vols (Paris, 1961-63).

Demetz, Peter, *René Rilkes Prager Jahre* (Düsselfdorf, 1953).

Engelhardt, Hartmut (ed.), *Materialen zu Rainer Maria Rilke, 'Die Aufzeichnungen des Malte Laurids Brigge'* (Frankfurt am Main, 1974).

Friedrich, Hugo, *Die Struktur der modernen Lyrik* (Hamburg, 1956).

Fuerst, Norbert, *Phases of Rilke* (Bloomington, 1958).

Fülleborn, Ulrich, *Das Strukturproblem der späten Lyrik Rilkes. Voruntersuchung zu einem historischen Rilke-Verständnis*, second edition (Heidelberg, 1973).

Goertz, Hartmann, *Frankreich und das Erlebnis der Form im Werke Rainer Maria Rilkes* (Stuttgart, 1932).

Goll, Claire, *Rilke et les femmes* (Paris, 1955).

Gray, Ronald, *The German Tradition in Literature 1871-1945* (Cambridge, 1965).

Guardini, Romano, *Rainer Maria Rilkes Deutung des Daseins. Eine Interpretation der Duineser Elegien* (Munich, 1953).

Hamburger, Käte (ed.), *Rilke in neuer Sicht* (Stuttgart, 1971).

Hartman, Geoffrey, *The Unmediated Vision. An Interpretation of Wordsworth, Hopkins, Rilke and Valéry,* second edition (New York, 1966).

Heerikhuizen, F.W. van, *Rainer Maria Rilke. His Life and Work,* translated by F. Renier and A. Cliff (New York, 1952).

Heller, Erich, *The Disinherited Mind. Essays in modern German literature and thought,* third edition (London, 1971).

Holthusen, Hans Egon, *Der späte Rilke* (Zürich, 1949).

Holthusen, Hans Egon, 'Rainer Maria Rilkes letzte Jahre', in *Der unbehauste Mensch* (Munich, 1951).

Kramer-Lauff, Dietgard, *Tanz und Tänzerisches in Rilkes Lyrik* (Munich, 1969).

Lang, Renée, *Rilke, Gide et Valéry* (Boulogne, 1953).

Lang, Renée, 'Rilke and his French contemporaries', *Comparative Literature,* 10 (1958), 136-43.

Lang, Renée, 'Ein fruchtbringendes Mißverständnis: Rilke und Valéry', *Symposium,* 13 (1959), 51-62.

Leishman, J.B., *Rainer Maria Rilke. 'Sonnets to Orpheus'* (London, 1957).

Loock, Wilhelm, *Rainer Maria Rilke. 'Die Aufzeichnungen des Malte Laurids Brigge'* (Munich, 1971).

Luke, F.D., 'Metaphor and Thought in Rilke's *Duino Elegies*', *Oxford German Studies,* 2 (1967), 110-28.

Mason, Eudo C., *Rilke* (Edinburgh/London, 1963).

Mason, Eudo C., *Lebenshaltung und Symbolik bei Rainer Maria Rilke,* second edition (Oxford, 1964).

Meyer, Herman, 'Die Verwandlung des Sichtbaren. Die Bedeutung der modernen bildenden Kunst für Rilkes späte Dichtung', in *Zarte Empirie. Studien zur Literaturgeschichte* (Stuttgart, 1963), pp. 287-334.

Mörchen, Hermann, *Rilkes Sonette an Orpheus* (Stuttgart, 1958).

Rolleston, James, *Rilke in Transition. An Exploration of his earliest poetry* (New Haven/London, 1970).

Ryan, Judith, *Umschlag und Verwandlung. Poetische Struktur und Dichtungstheorie in R.M. Rilkes Lyrik der mittleren Periode* (Munich, 1972).

Salis, J.R. von, *Rainer Maria Rilkes Schweizer Jahre. Ein Beitrag zur Biographie von Rilkes Spätzeit,* third edition (Frauenfeld, 1952).

Shaw, Priscilla Washburn, *Rilke, Valéry and Yeats. The Domain of the Self* (New Brunswick, 1964).

Smith, Peter, 'Elements of Rilke's Creativity', *Oxford German Studies*, 2 (1967), 129-48.

St. Hélier, Monique, 'Souvenir', in *Rilke et la France. Essais et Souvenirs* (Paris, 1942), pp. 233-236.

Stahl, E.L., *Creativity. A Theme from 'Faust' and the 'Duineser Elegien'* (Oxford, 1961).

Stahl, E.L., *Rainer Maria Rilkes 'Duineser Elegien'* (Oxford, 1965).

Steiner, Jacob, *Rilkes 'Duineser Elegien'*, second edition (Bern, 1969).

Stephens, Anthony, 'The Problem of Completeness in Rilke's Poetry 1922-26', *Oxford German Studies*, 4 (1969), 155-87.

Stephens, Anthony, *Rainer Maria Rilke's 'Gedichte an die Nacht'. An Essay in Interpretation* (Cambridge, 1972).

Wais, Karin, *Studien zu Rilkes Valéry-Übertragungen* (Tübingen, 1967).

Wood, Frank, *Rainer Maria Rilke. The Ring of Forms* (Minneapolis, 1958).

D. WORKS ON VALÉRY

(See also works by Bowra, Crasnow, Hartman and Shaw under C.)

Aigrisse, Gilberte, *Psychanalyse de Paul Valéry* (Paris, 1964).

Austin, L.J., 'La Genèse du "Cimetière marin"', *Cahiers de l'Association internationale des études françaises*, 3-5 (1953), 235-69.

Austin, L.J., 'Paul Valéry: Teste ou Faust?', *Cahiers de l'Association internationale des études françaises*, 17 (1965), 245-56.

Bémol, Maurice, *Paul Valéry* (Paris/Clermont-Ferrand, 1949).

Bémol, Maurice, *Variations sur Valéry*, 2 vols (Paris, 1952, 1959).

Berne-Joffroy, André, *Valéry* (Paris, 1960).

Chisholm, A.R., *An Approach to 'La Jeune Parque'* (Melbourne, 1938).

Cohen, Gustave, *Essai d'explication du 'Cimetière marin'* (Paris, 1946).

Crow, Christine M., *Paul Valéry. Consciousness and Nature* (Cambridge, 1972).

Daniel, V.J., *Paul Valéry: 'Eupalinos' and 'L'Ame et la danse'* (Oxford, 1967).

Duchesne-Guillemin, Jacques, *Études pour un Paul Valéry* (Neuchâtel, 1964).

Duchesne-Guillemin, Jacques, *Études de 'Charmes' de Paul Valéry* (Brussels, 1947).

Fehr, A.J.A., *Les dialogues antiques de Paul Valéry* (Leiden, 1960).

Gaède, E., *Nietzsche et Valéry: essai sur la comédie de l'esprit* (Paris, 1962).

Henry, A., *Langage et poésie chez Paul Valéry* (Paris, 1952).

Hytier, Jean, *La Poétique de Valéry* (Paris, 1953).

Hytier, Jean, 'Étude de la *Jeune Parque*', in *Questions de littérature. Études valéryennes et autres* (New York/London, 1967), pp. 3-39.

Ince, W.N., *The Poetic Thoery of Paul Valéry - inspiration and technique* (Leicester, 1961).

Köhler, Hartmut, *Poésie et profondeur sémantique dans la 'Jeune Parque' de Paul Valéry* (Nancy, 1965).

Köhler, Hartmut, *Paul Valéry: Dichtung und Erkenntnis. Das lyrische Werk im Lichte der Tagebücher* (Bonn, 1976).

Laurenti, Huguette (ed.), *Paul Valéry. Lectures de 'Charmes'* (Paris, 1974).

Laurette, P., *Le Thème de l'arbre chez Paul Valéry* (Paris, 1967).

Lawler, J.R., *Lecture de Valéry. Une Étude de 'Charmes'* (Paris, 1963).

Lawler, J.R., *The Poet as Analyst. Essays on Paul Valéry* (Berkeley/London, 1974).

Maurer, K., *Interpretationen zur späteren Lyrik Paul Valérys* (Munich, 1954).

Martin, Graham Dunstan, *Paul Valéry: 'Le Cimetière marin'* (Edinburgh, 1971).

McKay, Agnes, *The Universal Self. A Study of Paul Valéry* (London, 1961).

Noulet, Emile, *Paul Valéry (Études)* (Brussels, 1951).

Noulet, Emile (ed.), *Entretiens sur Paul Valéry* (Paris/The Hague, 1968).

Parent, Monique et Jean Levaillant (eds.), *Paul Valéry contemporain* (Paris, 1974).

Parisier-Plottel, J., *Les dialogues de Paul Valéry* (Paris, 1960).

Pire, François, *La Tentation du sensible chez Paul Valéry* (Paris, 1964).

Raymond, Marcel, *Paul Valéry et la tentation de l'esprit* (Neuchâtel, 1946 and 1964).

Robinson, Judith, *L'analyse de l'esprit dans les Cahiers de Valéry* (Paris, 1963).

Scarfe, Francis, *The Art of Paul Valéry: a study in dramatic monologue* (London, 1954).

Sewell, Elizabeth, *Paul Valéry. The Mind in the Mirror* (Cambridge, 1952).

Soulairol, J., *Paul Valéry* (Paris, 1952).

Suckling, Norman, *Paul Valéry and the Civilised Mind* (London, 1954).

Sutcliffe, *La Pensée de Paul Valéry* (Paris, 1955).

Thomson, Alastair, *Valéry* (Edinburgh/London, 1965).

Walzer, Pierre-Olivier, *La Poésie de Valéry* (Geneva, 1953).

Weinberg, Bernard, 'Valéry, *Le Cimetière marin*', in *The Limits of Symbolism. Studies of Five Modern French Poets* (Chicago, 1966).

Whiting, C.G., *Valéry jeune poète* (Paris, 1960).

Whiting, C.G., *Paul Valéry: 'Charmes ou Poèmes'* (London, 1973).

Wills, Ludmilla M., *Le Regard contemplatif chez Valéry et Mallarmé* (Amsterdam, 1974).

E. OTHER WORKS CITED

Bloom, Harold, *The Anxiety of Influence. A Theory of Poetry* (New York/London, 1973).

Laing, R.D., *The Divided Self. An Existential Study in Sanity and Madness* (London, 1965).

Poulet, Georges, *Études sur le temps humain*, I (Paris, 1972).

Salingar, L.G., 'T.S. Eliot. Poet and Critic', in *Pelican Guide to English Literature*, VII (London, 1961).

Stevens, Wallace, *Collected Poems* (London, 1955).

PUBLICATIONS OF THE INSTITUTE OF GERMANIC STUDIES

1   *Union List of Periodicals* dealing with Germanic languages and literatures in the University Library and in libraries of the colleges and institutes of the University
ISBN 0 85457 005 5   58 pp.   1956   out of print

2   *Schiller Bicentenary Lectures,* ed. by F. Norman
ISBN 0 85457 010 1   x, 168 pp.   1960   £10.50

3   *Schiller in England 1787–1960: a bibliography,* ed. by R. Pick
ISBN 0 85457 012 8   xvi, 123 pp.   1961   £8.15

4   *Theses in Germanic Studies 1903–61,* ed. by F. Norman
ISBN 0 85457 015 2   viii, 46 pp.   1962   £1.90

5   *Hofmannsthal Studies in Commemoration,* ed. by F. Norman
ISBN 0 85457 018 7   xii, 147 pp.   1963   £10.50

6   *Hauptmann Centenary Lectures,* ed. by K. G. Knight and F. Norman
ISBN 0 85457 021 7   167 pp.   1964   £10.50

7   *Essays in German Literature,* ed. by F. Norman
ISBN 0 85457 023 3   viii, 166 pp.   1965   £10.50

8   *Medieval German Studies* for F. Norman, ed. by A. T. Hatto and M. O'C. Walshe (reprint of 1965 edition)
ISBN 0 85457 057 8   x, 302 pp.   1973   £14.00

9   *German Language and Literature: select bibliography of reference books,* by L. M. Newman
Second enlarged edition
ISBN 0 85457 077 2   x, 175 pp.   1979   £2.50

10 *Theses in Germanic Studies 1962–67,* ed. by S. S. Prawer and V. J. Riley
ISBN 0 85457 032 2   vi, 18 pp.   1968   £1.25

11 *Probleme mittelalterlicher Überlieferung und Textkritik — Oxforder Colloquium 1966,* hrsg. von P. F. Ganz und W. Schröder (in collaboration with Erich Schmidt Verlag, Berlin)
ISBN 0 85457 033 0   196 pp.   1968   £10.75

12 *Essays in German Language, Culture and Society,* ed. by S. S. Prawer, R. Hinton Thomas, and L. W. Forster
ISBN 0 85457 036 5   x, 244 pp.   1969   £14.00

13 *Probleme mittelhochdeutscher Erzählformen — Marburger Colloquium 1969,* hrsg. von P. F. Ganz und W. Schröder (in collaboration with Erich Schmidt Verlag, Berlin)
ISBN 0 85457 048 9   287 pp.   1972   £15.25

14 *Goethe and the Scientific Tradition,* by H. B. Nisbet
ISBN 0 85457 050 0   xii, 83 pp.   1972   £7.00

15 *Essays in German and Dutch Literature,* ed. by W. D. Robson-Scott
ISBN 0 85457 051 9   viii, 191 pp.   1973   £13.50

16 *Three Essays on the 'Hildebrandslied',* by F. Norman, ed. by A. T. Hatto
ISBN 0 85457 052 7   x, 84 pp.   1973   £7.00

17 *Theses in Germanic Studies 1967–72,* ed. by W. D. Robson-Scott and V. J. Riley
ISBN 0 85457 055 1   vi, 18 pp.   1973   £1.20

18 *Stefan George: Dokumente seiner Wirkung. Aus dem Friedrich Gundolf Archiv der Universität London,* hrsg. von L. Helbing und C. V. Bock mit K. Kluncker (in collaboration with Castrum Peregrini, Amsterdam)
ISBN 0 85457 060 8   318 pp.   1974   £12.75

19 *Studien zur frühmittelhochdeutschen Literatur — Cambridger Colloquium 1971,* hrsg. von L. P. Johnson, H.-H. Steinhoff und R. A. Wisbey (in collaboration with Erich Schmidt Verlag, Berlin)
ISBN 0 85457 062 4   359 pp.   1974   £20.15

20 *Selected Essays on Medieval German Literature,* by K. C. King, ed. by J. L. Flood and A. T. Hatto
ISBN 0 85457 063 2   x, 219 pp.   1975   £13.50

21 *Althochdeutsche Glossen zum Alten Testament,* hrsg. von H. Thoma (in collaboration with Max Niemeyer Verlag, Tübingen)
ISBN 0 85457 067 5   xiv, 28 pp.   1975   out of stock

22 *Deutsche Literatur des späten Mittelalters — Hamburger Colloquium 1973,* hrsg. von W. Harms und L. P. Johnson (in collaboration with Erich Schmidt Verlag, Berlin)
ISBN 0 85457 068 3   315 pp.   1975   £19.00

23 *Germanistik in Festschriften von den Anfängen (1877) bis 1973.* In Zusammenarbeit mit dem Institute of Germanic Studies bearb. von Ingrid Hannich-Bode und Siegmund Heidelberg (in collaboration with J. B. Metzlersche Verlagsbuchhandlung, Stuttgart)
ISBN 0 85457 072 1   xii, 441 pp.   1976   out of stock

24 *Karl und Hanna Wolfskehl: Briefwechsel mit Friedrich Gundolf, 1899–1931,* hrsg. von K. Kluncker (in collaboration with Castrum Peregrini, Amsterdam)
ISBN 0 85457 074 8   319, 349 pp.   1977   £26.80
                            (2 vols.)   (plus postage)

25 *August Stramm: Kritische Essays und unveröffentlichtes Quellenmaterial aus dem Nachlass des Dichters,* hrsg. von J. D. Adler und J. J. White (in collaboration with Erich Schmidt Verlag, Berlin)
ISBN 0 85457 078 0   208 pp.   1979   £11.00

LIBRARY PUBLICATIONS

Hugo von Hofmannsthal-Ausstellung Katalog
ISBN 0 85457 013 6   32 pp.   1961   available on application (s.a.e.)
Gerhart Hauptmann Exhibition: catalogue prepared by H. F. Garten
ISBN 0 85457 016 0   22 pp.   1962

Periodical Holdings 1970
ISBN 0 85457 038 1   92 pp.   1970   £0.90

Periodical Holdings (supplements 1971–1973 supplied gratis with *Periodical Holdings 1970*)

German-language Literary and Political Periodicals, 1960–1974
ISBN 0 85457 064 0   60 pp.   1975   £1.90

Theses in Progress at British Universities, with work published in 1978 and work due to be published in 1979, as known on 1 January 1979
ISBN 0 85457 089 6   iv, 40 pp.   1979   £1.80
(previous lists — 1967 onwards, except 1973/74 issue, which is out of print — available on application)

An Outline Guide to Resources for the study of German language and literature in National, University and other libraries in the United Kingdom
ISBN 0 85457 084 5   vi, 53 pp.   1978   £1.00

Prices, which are for U.K. only, include postage, and are effective from 1 January 1979. They are liable to adjustment without notice. For overseas orders, add 20% to the price quoted.

This list, which supersedes all previous lists, is based on current stock.

All publications are obtainable on application to the Institute of Germanic Studies, 29 Russell Square, London WC1B 5DP.

BITHELL SERIES OF DISSERTATIONS

E.T.A. Hoffmann and the rhetoric of terror, by Elizabeth Wright
ISBN 0 85457 087 X   viii, 307 pp.   1979   £8.00

The second and third volumes are in the press:
Figures of transformation: Rilke and the example of Valéry, by R. F. Cox
Names and nomenclature in Goethe's 'Faust', by Ann White

The following are in preparation:
Landscape and landscape imagery in R. M. Rilke, by J. E. Sandford
The authority of the source of Middle High German narrative poetry, by C. Lofmark